*I will my book
to the God Indwelling,
Thy will.
It is done!*

Acknowledgments

IT HAS TAKEN TEN YEARS of thinking about writing, and six months of actual writing to complete this book. I would like to thank my husband, Ray, for his willingness to love me and to back me up in the middle of our own personal life changes, and then to hang on tightly as my writing this book created an additional emotional roller coaster ride. Thank you, Ray, for causing me to grow, and for being courageous enough to grow also.

In appreciation to Cindy, my daughter, for being a loving friend who encouraged me to keep writing, and for being strong enough to tell me when what I was saying in the book was not clear. Cindy, you were right!

Thanks, son, for allowing me to share in my book some of our life experiences together that were difficult to live through. You may have chosen me this life, Allen, and thanks for staying with it long enough to get to know me. Let's keep learning together!

To Susan Kovalik and Karen Olsen: Thanks for freely giving your time for my book with unconditional love during the time when it was difficult to give. Thanks to you I learned I could write, I learned how to use a computer, and learned how to be a child . . . all in two days?!! Thank you!

To Nancy and Paul Clemens for believing in me, encouraging me, then backing it up with the publishing of my book. Thanks Paul, for the many hours of patience and caring you gave in order to make sure my words were clear. Nancy, for your help in the beginning by reminding me that beautiful ultra-sensitives like you need this information.

Thanks too to my special friends Joe Kimm, Jr., Phyllis Kimm, Barbara Viebrock, Donna Ulery, Vimala Rodgers, Cindy Calhoun, Allen Calhoun, Ray Calhoun, Bill Clifford, Paul Clemens, Nancy Clemens, Laura Frisch, and David Marshall for reviewing my book or listening and giving personal insight to make it better.

Thank you, Vimala, for putting your heart and soul and many hours into my book at a time when it couldn't have been more difficult for you, editing my words to make them into understandable English, in the vocabulary of this planet. Also, Vim, for keeping the essence of me in my book.

To all the ultra-sensitives in my classes and workshops, and to my clients: Thank you for helping me to understand my sensitivity more clearly so I can continue to help ultra-sensitives. As I grow to love you more, I can learn to love myself more. There is no greater gift you could give me. How small the words "Thank You" seem.

Last, but not least, I would like to express my love and appreciation to Dr. Eugene Whitworth for teaching me and giving me a powerful foundation to live by and for creating the opportunity for me to learn how to release a father figure, a teacher, a friend . . . and leave home.

M.C.

Contents

Introduction

THIS BOOK IS designed for you to use whenever you need it and whatever you need it for, and not necessarily in sequence. If sequence is important, then I will specify (to do that) particular work in sequence for the best result. Do not let anyone take away your right to make up your own mind, even with the exercises in this book. Use them in the way they work best for you.

Create a notebook especially for your ultra-sensitivity work. Choose a notebook that fits your needs. Be as brief or as detailed in your written expression as you want to be. This is a notebook for you and no one else to see or read unless you want to show it to them. Do the exercises only when you need to clarify something about your ultra-sensitivity. Do not feel guilty if you do not write in your notebook for six days or six months. **Just use your notebook when you need it.**

Within this book there are many times when I italicize a word or words. In explaining about ultra-sensitivity, many times the way a word or phrase is regularly used is not the way I want you to think about it. I want you to put these words in a new context other than their accepted uses. I have italicized certain words because I want you to add a new dimension to them.

I use the phrase *picked up* to mean that you have added something extra into your being that you may or may not want. It means you have *picked up* information/feelings/physical pain/emotions that have entered into your *communication center*. I want you to have an awareness of what is incoming and outgoing in emotional content as well as in energy. I want you to have an awareness of exactly who you are, so at any given second you will know if anything foreign or anything that is not truly a part of you has entered your own *communication center* (body/mind/emotions/spirit).

The reasons I have put slashes between words is to alert you to the fact that all the words used are needed to explain fully the concept I am using. Like the phrase *communication center*. Your *communication center* consists of information from your body, information from your mind, information from your emotions and information from your spirit. Sometimes one or more words are needed to explain ultra-sensitivity, so I have used slashes to create a meaning that has more information than any one word I could use.

Throughout this book I will use different words that to me describe the God Energy, in order to explain the pure energy that is God. I will refer to the Universal

Self that is within all of us. I also like to use *Divine Self* or *Divine Energy* because it is the same energy within all things.

Because I want to honor all people's beliefs, I have used many different ways to describe God. Many different religions have their own way of describing the omnipresent God Energy and I honor their right to believe as they do. I appreciate everyone giving me the same respect to believe in God in my own personal way. I also honor a person's right not to believe in God.

My goal in life is to help ultra-sensitives find a deeper understanding of what their sensitivity is for, and how they can help themselves. Ultra-sensitives can also help the people around them by helping them to recognize their ultra-sensitivity. It is important for you to know that your mind *communication center*—brain/mind/emotion/spirit—is a wonderful tool and that everything that comes into your *communication center* is VALID. When you think thoughts, they are there for a reason and they have some meaning or connection to you.

ALL YOUR THOUGHTS ARE VALID.
ALL YOUR THOUGHTS ARE IN YOUR MIND
FOR A REASON.

This is true even if you are *picking up* thoughts from someone else because they are thinking about you at the time. Even the craziest and most unrelated thoughts have validity. You have to figure out how they fit into your life. There are sensitives who drive along the highway and have destructive thoughts come into their mind that are entirely foreign to their life and their way of thinking. They may have been concerned about someone they cared about who had just said he did not want to live anymore, and although the sensitive did not hear the words spoken, she *picked it up.* There is always a valid reason for the thoughts that come into your *communication center.*

1 *What is an Ultra-Sensitive?*

HOW MANY TIMES have you heard the words, "You're too sensitive for your own good," or the other classic negative statement, "You're just too sensitive?" I don't agree with either statement because you are just as sensitive as you are supposed to be. Your ultra-sensitivity is a positive and powerful way that you can help yourself to be a more fully expressive person, even though at this point in time it may seem that you are your own worst enemy. It may be that you do not know how to use your ultra-sensitivity for your own benefit or for the benefit of others. You are meant to own your *complete ultra-sensitivity* in order to help you define and structure yourself, as well as the world you live in. Do not allow others to structure you, but learn to structure yourself with true understanding of your ultra-sensitivity.

Ultra-sensitivity is an acquired talent or skill that can be learned by anyone through one life or many lifetimes. Balanced, centered ultra-senstives are the next step in the evolution of humankind. It is everyone's positive destiny to be a centered, balanced awakened ultra-sensitive, if and when they choose to awaken their ultra-sensitivity.

All people are sensitive. Some people are ultra-sensitive. There are even a few extreme ultra-sensitives who have difficulty existing in life at all. Many times I will describe "ultra-sensitivity" in the extreme. You will need to find where *your* ultra-sensitivity fits in. Even though I will describe ultra-sensitivity in a variety of ways, you need to tailor the information by selecting the information that fits you; then you will have found an exact description of your individual ultra-sensitivity.

When you find a piece of information that you agree is a trait of yours, write it down in your notebook as you read. When you have completed reading this book, you should have a definite individual description of your ultra-sensitivity.

All ultra-sensitives amplify or magnify all information incoming and outgoing from their actions/feelings/thoughts/brain/mind/spirit, which is their *communication center*. They usually feel/believe that the experience they are having in the moment will remain the way it is forever, be it positive or negative. Frequently an ultra-sensitive experience can be overwhelming and often disruptive to ordinary life events.

As an ultra-sensitive you experience feelings, thoughts and sensations that cannot be explained by logic or your past experiences. There are three areas in which these occur: **emotional, physical** and **intuitive**.

Emotional ultra-sensitivity is the ability to feel what other people are feeling as if those feelings were your very own.

Physical ultra-sensitivity is the ability to feel in your body what someone else is feeling. Sometimes you will feel exactly what they are feeling. Sometimes you will experience more pain than the persons you are *picking up* from, because they are used to their level of pain and you are not. Since you are not used to their level of pain, you will often experience their pain more deeply than they do themselves.

I DO NOT WISH TO EXPERIENCE THIS AT THIS TIME

If at any time you do not wish to experience anything, then just speak up and say, "I DO NOT WISH TO EXPERIENCE THIS AT THIS TIME." It has the strongest impact if you speak it out loud.

1. Say it as many times as you need to say it.
2. Say it until the experience stops.
3. Say your name to calm and strengthen yourself.
4. Say your name again to fill the space you emptied.
5. Say your name again to stabilize your world.
6. Keep saying your name until you feel safe, relaxed and complete.

If you say, "I do not wish to experience this at this time," it gives you the opportunity to call this experience back to you **IF** and **WHEN** you do want the

SAY WHAT YOU MEAN
AND MEAN WHAT YOU SAY

experience. Learn to use the power of your words. **Say what you mean and mean what you say.** At first it takes time to speak with meaning, knowing exactly the meaning of the words you are using. This is basic to controlling and directing your sensitivity for positive outcomes for yourself and others.

Intuitive ultra-sensitivity is the ability to experience visions, prophetic information, spaces and dimensions that are not yet recognized by science; also **psychometry**, the ability of touching things and reading their past as well as their future history, or by the use of a person's name, reading a person's present life history without any prior information.

Healing is also included in *intuitive ultra-sensitivity* because the healer can read/feel/experience the present condition of the body. If the ill health condition is not changed, the healer can read/feel/ experience to what degree it can progress in the final stages. The healer can also give information on how to change habits and patterns in order to create strong health. Everything can be changed with the willingness of the person to change. The healer can also read what the initial cause is for the condition with very little or no feedback.

All types of ultra-sensitives receive messages from everyone and everything that relates to what they are experiencing at the time. If ultra-sensitives are wide open, they will receive more varied information. If they are looking for a specific thing, they will be open only to their area of interest. As an example, if they are interested in buying a specific kind of computer, then in their daily travels they will be alert to all kinds of information that has a connection to their thoughts about purchasing a new computer. They will be more aware of the kind of computer they want to buy, and they will see it in the offices where they do business. They may have hardly noticed it before they had an interest in that particular computer. They have emotionally attuned their mind to that specific information and their *communication center* is directing them to the information they are seeking.

WRITTEN GOALS CHANGE YOUR LIFE
TO THE POSITIVE

When asking, you do not always have to ask verbally to get an answer or solution. When you ask with your thoughts, you also receive answers.

Another way to receive answers is through the method of WRITING YOUR GOALS DOWN. **Setting written goals is important towards having your life change and move forward.** If you do not set written goals, you are asking for the same thing that is happening today to happen tomorrow. If you do not set new *written* goals when you are going through a painful experience, that experience will continue until you, another person, circumstances, or events change it. New written goals that you put your will and desire into will attract people or information to you that will cause changes to happen in your life, career, or personal relationships.

Most ultra-sensitives live their lives with their ultra-sensitivity wide open, and for that reason do not like to be in large crowds. Often it is painful for an ultra-sensitive to visit a friend in the hospital. There is a deep desire within ultra-sensitives to help all the people around them that are in emotional or physical pain. For this reason it is sometimes difficult for them even to read the newspaper or hear the news on television. When sensitives are awakening their ultra-sensitivity, they will also become ultra-sensitive to many things that did not affect them before. The newspaper or TV news are good examples. There is a sense within them of being "different" that is not stated; they just feel it all around them.

The feeling of being "alien" or "set apart" is a frequent occurrence that invades ultra-sensitives sometimes when they are with friends and sometimes when they are in a group of people. It is as if suddenly they are in an entirely different culture they do not understand. For example: If three people are visiting together and two of the people are sharing a private joke, the third person is feeling isolated or left out because s/he is not a part of the experience that happened to create the private joke. The third person feels alien, left out, and totally alone. If the third person (the ultra-sensitive) could understand at that moment that s/he can create her/his *own* history with both people, then s/he can in fact be a part of anything s/he truly wants to be a part of at any time s/he chooses to become involved.

SENSITIVITY IS MORE THAN
A SORE POINT

Ultra-sensitives usually understand the people around them, but they do not always understand themselves and their own differences. There are times when ultra-sensitives feel/see/know the sense of being in their body looking out their eyes with the same reality they have when they are sitting inside a car looking out the windshield of the car. Even in a meeting there can be a feeling of being outside looking in. It is often acknowledged among ultra-sensitives that there is a sensation within them that there is something important that they should be doing, that they have a destiny to follow, and even though they are not sure what that is, it is something that is just out of reach, and it is evading their conscious thoughts.

The feeling can persist that no matter what you do or accomplish, it is never going to be enough. When the ultra-sensitive is having problems, the feeling that they "do not fit in" often returns, and when it does return it continues to haunt the ultra-sensitive. When this feeling happens it means that there is something inside the sensitive, inside her/his universe—body, mind, emotions, spirit—that does not belong, and it is creating an imbalance that gives the ultra-sensitive the feeling that everything is going wrong in her/his life.

The feeling of fear sometimes overwhelms ultra-sensitives to the point that they are afraid to move or do anything. Most of the time ultra-sensitives do not recognize it as fear, and it will manifest itself as a blanket of non-caring, depression or boredom. When it does manifest as fear, it feels as if the fear in you, the ultra-sensitive, will never go away.

All these feelings, and many more, are the ways an ultra-sensitive experiences life. As soon as they understand themselves and their abilities, their lives can be confident, complete, healthy, happy and full of richly rewarding experiences.

All people have the opportunity to develop their sensitivity to the point where they can become healthy, well-adjusted ultra-sensitives, taking their place in the world. There is a purpose for being ultra-sensitive. You can develop your ultra-sensitivity without going through the deep pain most ultra-sensitives experience in their lives.

In order to develop your ultra-sensitivity, you can open up your emotional self a little at a time, taking steps to learn about yourself and your relationship to the world you live in. Remember that being ultra-sensitive does not mean being out of control emotionally. True ultra-sensitives have more information available to them to live their lives than non-ultra-sensitives, because they have a multi-leveled awareness of themselves, the people they love, and this planet they live on.

You do not have to be a victim of your ultra-sensitivity. There are many proven techniques available that can help you create your life to become a safe, expanding, challenge. The very reason your sensitivity is within you is a signal that you are gifted in a very special way that was meant to make you strong, not weak. You always have a choice and the right to choose. How you choose is up to you. Remember that even in not choosing you are making a choice not to move.

**NOT MAKING A CHOICE IS STILL A CHOICE.
IT IS A CHOICE TO STAY WHERE YOU ARE.**

Techniques to Bring Out, Enhance, or Balance Your Ultra-sensitivity

1. **Listen to your words**; they are creating your life.
2. **Trust yourself** and trust what you feel/know/ see.
3. **Make a commitment** to be seen and visible.
4. **Be who you are.**
5. **Ask for what you want.**
6. **Respect other ultra-sensitives** even if they have not achieved as much as you have.
7. **Do not judge** yourself or others.

EXERCISES

Write the answers to these questions in your notebook.

1. What **Negative word or statement** am I using that I want to remove from my vocabulary? (Just pick a word or statement that you no longer want to say in your life—then, to the best of your ability, stop using it.)

2. In what way did I **trust myself** today? (Remember—small ways are as important to your development as major, earth-shaking ones.) Or in what way did I **not trust myself?**

3. What action did I take today that made me **visible and seen? Invisible and unseen?**

4. What did I do today when someone wanted me to be **the way they wanted me to be?** Did I remain who I am, or did I become who they wanted?

5. In what way did I **ask** for what I wanted today? Or **not ask?**

6. In what way did I **show respect** to other ultra-sensitives, whether they returned that respect or not? Or how did I not show respect?

7. How have I **reinforced my right** to be ultra-sensitive today? Or how did I deny my ultra-sensitivity?

8. How have I **gone beyond judgment** of others today and not judged? Or how have I judged others?

9. How have I **received** today in word, thought, deed or action when it was hard for me to receive? Or how have I **given?**

2 *Owning Control of Your Life*

THE FIRST STEP toward owning control of your life is to create a structure or foundation that will show you how to start understanding why you are on this earth. It is important for you to know where you are at this very moment.

Begin with an inventory of your positive traits. Remember that you and everyone else have been taking an inventory of your negative traits as long as you can remember. This is more than positive thinking. This is the time that you need to take the following action for yourself:

1. Create an inventory of your **positive traits.**
2. Ask a loving, **objective friend** to look at your actions and reactions to life.
3. Find your **talents.**

Do not overwhelm yourself at first. Take one step at a time. You will have all the time you need to do everything you want to do. The first and most important thing is that you are now starting.

4. If you do not have a friend around whom you trust and like, then seek a **counselor** who you feel truly understands you.
5. Seek someone to help you see what kind of raw material you are beginning with, the **raw material called "you,"** and how you can use this raw material and re-form yourself to change your life.
6. Remember that the only person who is going to make a difference in your life is **you.**
7. Use **care** in identifying support. If you find someone who tells you how wrong you are, without providing useful information and encouragement to help you change, then that is **NOT** the right person to help you.

WHY DID YOU GO THROUGH WHAT YOU WENT THROUGH IN CHILDHOOD?

Why did you go through what you went through in childhood?—to make some sense out of what has happened to you since you have been born. There is a rhyme and reason for all the circumstances and events that have happened in your life. One of the most important set of changes in your life occurs at puberty. Puberty is described as "the state of physical development when sexual reproduction first becomes possible:

the age of puberty is generally fixed in common law at fourteen for boys and twelve for girls."

Puberty is a time when young people are over-loaded with sensory information, intuitive as well as psychological/physical/sexual information. At this time there seem to be two unconscious choices available to choose from: *structural* or *conceptual.*

The words *structural* and *conceptual* define the way that ultra-sensitives relate to the world outside themselves as well as the way they relate to themselves. One unconscious choice can be a *structural* choice.

A *structural* choice is an acceptance generally to follow the rules and regulations that are presented, whether that means rules that parents set, rules that the school system sets, rules such as being on time—and the ability to say yes or no.

This usually means that the *structural* person has chosen to be physically active or academically active as a structure to work within. This focus gives young persons a structure to live life from in a way that relates or correlates all the new information that is coming into their *communication center* (body/mind/emo-tions/spirit).

The other unconscious choice is the *conceptual.* This is the choice of living your life with emotional ideas but no framework, details, and little or no connection to a logical sequence of thoughts (events). To me the *conceptual* means that the young person will live life second-to-second by using her/his immediate feelings to make choices.

This choice for the young ultra-sensitive is a difficult one. There is no foundation to work from or boundaries to get feedback from. There is no present memory connected to the past actions—as far as what did work and what did not work the last time the same actions were tried. There is usually a sense of "I just know that it will be okay," or "I just know that it will work for me *this time.*" Conceptual ultra-sensitives can stop being called "wrong," or "not fitting in," and still be their own individual selves by creating an individual structure that works for them. They can also accept criticism about themselves without giving up who they are, because they can take the structure that everyone else lives by and individualize it to their own specifications.

So *conceptual* ultra-sensitives choose—without realizing they are making a choice—from the *conceptual* information that has little correlation with the physical reality/world they must live in. They are overloaded with sensory information because they do not have the definition that the *structural* person has available. They have made an unconscious choice not to relate to the structural world. With a *conceptual* ultra-sensitive, there is too much information and no cross-reference or other way to select or shut out any of the information.

Many times ultra-sensitives will choose something outside their experience to slow down or shut down the information, in order to gain some rest, acceptance, peace, quiet; they will use chemicals such as alcohol, refined sugar, chocolate, caffeine, food, drugs or other combinations of chemical substances. The choices are made very specifically by what chemicals are chosen so that the chemical choice will slow down or close down the specific area of ultra-sensitivity that the ultra-sensitive feels that s/he cannot cope with. Alcohol closes down the negative thoughts, feelings, sensations that are within ultra-sensitives, as well as the negative input that they are being bombarded with outside themselves.

Ultra-sensitives that have made the *conceptual* choice usually do not have methods available to stop or slow down the information that is coming into their brain/mind/emotions/spirit *communication center.* They get lost in what is right for everyone else versus what is right for them. Ultra-sensitives often feel that no one seems to understand them, yet many times they are rebelling against the very people that could help them. As a result, they lose their support system.

Ultra-sensitives that have chosen the *conceptual* way of living will keep working to understand why they are having painful experiences, but will not understand why they are unable to get out of the pain or see beyond the pain. They still do not have something to measure themselves with in the world. Ultra-sensitives try to get the answer to whatever problems they are having by turning to friends that are having the same problems they are. Each person they seek out will usually give them a different answer, and that will confuse them even more. Now they are even more unclear about what really works for them and what does not. At this point it seems hopeless. There is hope, however, if *conceptual* ultra-sensitives will seek out someone who will help them to trust themselves and clarify what they want from themselves and from the world.

The early unconscious decision to be either a *structural* or *conceptual* ultra-sensitive remains basically unchanged throughout the ultra-sensitive's life unless there is a life crisis or conscious awakening. When this happens, sensitives find themselves having to face, understand, and accept either the *structural* or *conceptual* knowledge . . . the one that is the opposite of the one they chose at puberty.

There is a natural tendency towards either the *conceptual* or *structural* choice and a definite unconscious choice at puberty that is determined on the part of sensitives by the deluge of sensory information flooding into them when they desperately need a structure or some frame of reference to make sense out of the sensory world they find themselves inundated with so they can survive. As long as they find a place or group to belong to, then they can survive. Life becomes one painful experience after another for ultra-sensitives who unconsciously chose the *conceptual* way of life and do not know how to align themselves with any structure. The lack of structure or understanding of themselves causes them to be forced around by circumstances and events outside themselves without a sense of belonging to anything or anyone including themselves. Remember—structure *can* be created by the *conceptual* ultra-sensitive *for* the *conceptual* ultra-sensitive into a complete understanding of how they are living as a result of this understanding. They need to continue developing it into a foundation to live their life by.

Conceptual ultra-sensitives must face and understand their structural side in order to be complete. They must learn how to work well within the framework of time (such as BEING on time) and must learn how to work well with money; they must learn how to relate to the physical world by being able to follow directions; they must learn how to accept and take care of their physical body. *Conceptual ultra-sensitives* must be accepted and receive the results of being successful in the material world without losing touch with their intuitive/spiritual side.

Some ultra-sensitives are motivated by their own creativity. This type of ultra-sensitive chooses an art career, dancing, singing, acting, painting, teaching, or music. When the ultra-sensitive picks this type of career, it usually satisfies her/his need for self-expression. This kind of choice helps the *conceptual ultra-sensitive* to find a creative structure that works.

Structural ultra-sensitives will live and work in the world, surviving and achieving, until a crisis surfaces in their life and then the structure they have built for themselves will no longer work for them. They are not only inflexible in the world, they are also inflexible within their own structure. They are unwilling (or do not know how) to make the changes that would cause them to grow.

Any structure that you build will work for you, as long as you do not try to have all-encompassing control in your life over everything and everyone, including yourself. If what you are doing is stifling or suffocating to yourself, your spiritual side will create a crisis to end the suffocating actions in your life.

All-encompassing control is against the natural order of things. There must be movement and willingness to move or the natural law of cause and effect will force movement by creating a crisis that creates change. That force comes from within you and not from outside of you. When you have continually said NO to change, that means you are going against the survival systems of body/mind/emotions/spirit. Then your life-support systems (body or mind or emotions or spirit or any combination of these systems) take over for your own survival, which forces you to move, no matter how painful that movement may be. It may occur either in a relationship, a career, or a family situation. The painful process of awakening will make you create movement. This movement will make you realize that what you have been doing is not working, and now you must face and understand your emotional (*conceptual*) side.

As this is true for the *structural ultra-sensitive* it is also true of the *conceptual ultra-sensitive*. An ultra-sensitive must learn to honor her/his "mirror side" no matter which way s/he chose at puberty, whether *conceptual* or *structural*; the other side of sensitivity must be experienced.

There are ultra-sensitive people who have achieved a creative balance between the *conceptual* and *structural* sides of themselves. They are able to reach from either side of their being, or to create a blend of both the *conceptual* and *structural*, for what they are doing at the time. That is why many times when a person is a genius in her/his field, that genius is many times eccentric. Her/his focus is on one thing and one thing almost totally. ALL of us can call on that genius side of ourselves without being so totally unbalanced. It takes a lot of work to keep seeking the natural balance within ourselves.

Our usual approach for achieving anything is to concentrate on that project until it is done, giving other people in our life little time or attention. The same is true of other projects. Usually when we give up this "one-mindedness," we lose our focus to complete the project we were working on. When working with a narrow perspective on a project that we feel strongly about, the very attitude we are determined to keep draws or magnetizes the opposite extreme into our life. As an example: When you know how something must be, and you leave no room for any variety or change, your structural attitude will automatically attract the very changes you were opposed to in the beginning.

We must always seek the natural balance in all things: activity, work, sleep, play or relationships. The natural order of things will not tolerate an imbalance, so if we do not listen we get dis-ease. Another way to say this is that we lose our "flow" or "ease" of life and cause a sickness in our body.

The second step toward owning control of your own life is to identify what kind of ultra-sensitive you are, in other words, what the source of your information as an ultra-sensitive is.

There are three kinds of ultra-sensitives:

1.   Visual
2.   Knowing
3.   Feeling

Visual ultra-sensitives experience predominantly through the awareness of seeing. They are visual learners. In the physical world *visual ultra-sensitives* relate to the world they live in by their sight. Many times when they understand something, *emotionally visual ultra-sensitives* will relate to their emotions by saying, "I see." In the intuitive area of their lives, *visual ultra-sensitives* may experience visions or see with their "mind's-eye" actual pictures that can be still or in action as they watch. *Visual ultra-sensitives* receive information better by seeing things in physical form such as words, pictures, visual action pictures, "minds-eye" pictures.

THOUGHTS ARE THE FIRST PHYSICAL FORM OF MANIFESTATION

Knowing ultra-sensitives are ultra-sensitives who *know*, but usually they do not know why they know or how they know—they just ***know***. Information may come through them without their even having the information consciously in their thoughts or present life experience.

It is difficult for *knowing ultra-sensitives* because they usually learn from knowledge or life experience through a logical sequence of information or events. It is sometimes difficult for *knowing ultra-sensitives* because they receive very little or no sensory input to back up their information. They may find that they are talking about things they have no present knowledge about, and may be surprised as they listen to the information that is coming through them, especially when it turns out to be true!

Feeling ultra-sensitives experience life through their feelings. They speak by saying, "I feel," when answering questions or giving information. *Feeling ultra-sensitives* feel what they feel, feel what people around them feel, feel for plants, animals, and the world. To feeling ultra-sensitives "feelings" are a tactile organ. "Feelings" is one organ with many different tentacles. Ultra-sensitives are tactile learners. They learn by touching others *with* their feelings and being touched *by* their feelings, as well as experiencing the feelings that others around them are experiencing. They use their feeling perceptions as a physical sensory organ to bring information into their *communication system*. *Feeling* ultra-sensitives love the textures of all things in life. Textures of soap bubbles, textures of silk, satin, the texture of the bark of a tree, the texture of someone else's feelings for the pet they love. A *feeling sensitive's* feelings are a physical/touching/sensory tool. When they feel something, it touches them.

Feeling ultra-sensitives can feel what has happened in the past experiences of any person, place, or thing. They can also sense what is coming into their lives and the lives of others. *Feeling ultra-sensitives* are usually filled with the emotions of the moment and many times may not be able to pull themselves out of their own emotions or the emotions they have *picked up* from other people.

Any of the three kinds of ultra-sensitives just described—*visual, knowing,* and *feeling*—can learn how to expand in a useful and positive way into the other kinds of ultra-sensitivity. Through practice of the techniques given throughout this book, ultra-sensitives of any type can develop all three kinds of ultra-sensitivity, which will make their ultra-sensitivity a more complete and balanced tool to use in their lives.

1. The Sponge Ultra-sensitive

Sponge ultra-sensitives absorb the feelings and sensations of all the people around them. They take on emotional connections, especially with people that they love or are frightened by. They usually have little control over what they are emotionally connected with, be it positive or negative. The exception is when they use their will for someone they love. Then they control their energy until they feel "complete" with what they were connected to.

They are released from an emotional tie only if the connection is broken by the other person. It can also be broken by having the *sponge ultra-sensitive* state his or her name until the connection is severed. *Sponge ultra-sensitives* love deeply whoever or whatever they love, and will defend that love with all their daily life energy. They will hold on to relationships that are painful, often past the time these relationships are positive experiences for them in their life.

The positive talent of *sponge ultra-sensitives* is that they have the ability for deep understanding of themselves, their loved ones, and life. They can connect with people on a deep level of experience. Once they bring their ultra-sensitivity under control, they make excellent counselors, teachers, or members of any profession that needs that depth of understanding.

2. The Vessel Ultra-sensitive

Vessel ultra-sensitives are filled selectively by what they choose to see, experience or recognize in their life.

Vessel ultra-sensitives make that choice by who or what they love or care deeply about and mainly *pick up* on those specific things or those specific people. Whatever is happening to the *vessel ultra-sensitive* in her/his own life, makes her/him sensitive to those who are experiencing the same things in their lives. The *vessel ultra-sensitive* is susceptible to *picking up* the same conditions or emotional problems that others are going through.

Vessel ultra-sensitives will experience the condition that is troubling someone else when the *vessel ultra-sensitive* has the "seed condition" within her or himself. That means that if *vessel ultra-sensitives* have back problems, heart problems, kidney problems, or relationship-breaking-up problems—no matter how large or small a problem—then they will most likely *pick up* a similar problem not only from someone they love, but from everyone they come into contact with—in person, on the phone, watching television, hearing about the person, touching a person in a store as they are passing by.

When this ultra-sensitivity is under control, *vessel ultra-sensitives* can store information within themselves for the moment and then release it without having any negative residues. A *vessel ultra-sensitive* can help others to see the many different potentials of any situation or event before, after, or during the time it is happening.

3. The Catalyst Ultra-sensitive

Catalyst ultra-sensitives are either creating change, entering someone's life when they are in change, entering a company that is on the brink of success or breaking up, or entering a person's life when s/he is about to face a crisis.

If you are this type of sensitive you might often wonder why people pass through your life instead of your being like many of your friends who have had the same friends since first grade. You are an ultra-sensitive who makes changes happen by just being there. People will re-enter your life whom you have not seen for years when some new changes are about to take place in their lives. You are the missing ingredient that heralds change for anything you enter, or for anyone's life you may enter.

A CATALYST SENSITIVE CREATES CHANGE BY JUST BEING THERE

If you are willing to change and accept changes in your own personal life, then your life will stay stable and constant even in the midst of your changes and the changes that you bring other people. It does not mean that you cannot have long term relationships in your life. It also does not mean that you must move from job to job.

What it DOES mean is that you must choose what you do best and find a job in which change is a part of, or the whole of, your job. It is true of many *catalyst ultra-sensitives* that in order to make major changes in their lives quite often they have to move physically from one house to another or from one location to another. The changes the *catalyst ultra-sensitive* creates in the lives of others eventually creates changes in her or his own life.

4. The Bridge Ultra-sensitive

Bridge ultra-sensitives create a place for other people to find, understand or follow. They are quite often pioneers in whatever field they choose as their occupation. They are inventive, creative, and usually talk about things that other people cannot always understand. This type of ultra-sensitive creates a way to reach this new place or new information, then rushes on to newer information and more new undiscovered or unexplored areas. The *bridge ultra-sensitive* is good at helping people work together by creating a unity in whatever project or group they are involved in.

**BRIDGE ULTRA-SENSITIVES CREATE WAYS TO
REACH NEW THOUGHTS, NEW IDEAS AND
NEW INFORMATION**

Bridge ultra-sensitives do not have patience with themselves in what they feel they SHOULD be doing but are NOT doing at the time. Many times you may find them as extroverts that feel they must make a difference in the world. They usually are very private people about their personal lives and are selective about who they share their life obstacles with.

Bridge ultra-sensitives can help others to see where they need to go next. They can give people the keys needed to reach the desired goal or objective. This ultra-sensitive, when set upon a course or a purpose, will not back up or retreat from the desired destination. Once this type of ultra-sensitive has made a commitment in helping you, s/he will not stop or back off until the goal is complete.

A NEGATIVE-POTENTIAL ULTRA-SENSITIVE IS NOT A NEGATIVE PERSON

---

5. The Negative-potential Ultra-sensitive

A *Negative-potential ultra-sensitive* is NOT a negative person. *Negative-potential ultra-sensitives* are ultra-sensitives who see/feel/hear/know the negative potential of every situation in life that they are emotionally involved in.

Their ultra-sensitivity even includes people they love, and not just themselves. With people they love, they also experience the negative potential happening to them. If they are riding in a car on a mountain road where they have any apprehension about anything in their life, they will experience every potential negative possibility of an accident on every curve they drive on, or as a passenger, on every curve they travel around. In traffic, if they have apprehension about anything in their life, including the traffic, they will experience every major or minor potential accident during the trip.

NEGATIVE-POTENTIAL ULTRA-SENSITIVES CAN MAKE THE POSITIVE POTENTIAL HAPPEN WITH ANYTHING THEY ARE INVOLVED IN OR WITH

Negative-potential ultra-sensitives can turn their talent around so they can experience understanding not just the *negative-potential* but the *positive-potential* in all things including themselves. They can then make the *positive-potential* happen in their lives. They can stop having to live with potential disasters every second of their lives. In sensing potential danger, this ultra-sensitive does not always put the information in the right place in connection with the right person. Usually they connect the danger with themselves or their loved ones, when many times it is information that is coming to them about someone they do not know or something else other than what they think it is connected to. For example, they may sense a plane crash. The information is valid but they connect it with themselves. They connect it with the plane trip THEY are taking instead of connecting it with the plane crash that is going to happen 2000 miles away. One out of one hundred times will the negative potential that is sensed by the *negative-potential ultra-sensitive* really happen to themselves or someone they know.

If *negative-potential ultra-sensitives* could clearly develop their talents so they could control and focus their senses, this kind of ultra-sensitivity could be of great help to humanity. They need to learn how to be able to say exactly where and when a disaster is going to happen. Then they could explain the percentage of the strength of the potential happening, and how strongly they felt it was going to happen. The answer to this sensitive's bringing this talent under control is in the use of concentration on a consistent basis with daily practice.

The best exercise for the development of concentration is the **White Door Exercise**:

1. Find a quiet moment. A quiet moment means when you are waiting for someone or something. Then quiet your mind. Your eyes do not have to be closed.

2. Picture a white door. It is in a door frame which is white also. It is standing by itself. It is plain, flat, smooth wood. It is painted white. There is a plain gold doorknob with no keyhole. The door is closed. It is in front of the universe filled with stars. You can see part of the universe around the sides of the door and door frame.

3. Set the alarm on your watch for three minutes. You can also set your mind to be aware if anyone needs your attention. The alarm is better because your mind will not worry about whether or not the time is up.

4. Do not let your mind think of anything but the white door. Every time your mind goes off on another thought bring it back to focus on the plain white door. I have picked a montonous, boring thing to concentrate on, on purpose. It is one of the ways that I know to reach that part of your mind that needs to develop concentration. Do not let the door open until you hear the alarm. Then open the door. This exercise develops your concentration.

Sometimes *negative-potential ultra-sensitives* are so overwhelmed by the fear that they will experience nausea or feel that they are going to pass out, or that this anxiety will be more than they can handle. They just want everything to stop or go away so they can rest for a little while. It is difficult for this type of ultra-sensitive to travel or be involved in anything that they cannot control. Usually there is a constant fear that they will put themselves into a situation they will not be able to stop. Agoraphobia is a negative extreme of this type of ultra-sensitivity.

6. The Blocked Ultra-sensitive

Blocked ultra-sensitives are ultra-sensitives who do not know how to relate to their sensitivity. They became blocked at some point in their life and for survival they have protected themselves by blocking their ultra-sensitive nature. They direct their life by depending on only their logical mind for direction. They do not see the value of their emotions.

They suppress their emotions from themselves as well as from others. These people are usually kind, thoughtful, generous, and reserved to everyone. They cannot express their deep emotions to the people that they are emotionally involved with, or they can express their emotions only after using alcohol or chemicals. They use the logical structure that is accepted by the material/ physical world as a blueprint to guide their life.

They are highly judgmental of themselves as well as of others, using judgment as a protective device to prevent any further pain to themselves. They do things for others by choosing who they feel really deserves their help. Then they give their time and energy beyond where most people would stop. Some *blocked ultra-sensitives* put other people before themselves so they have no unstructured leisure time; so, in fact, they do not have any leisure time at all.

They usually do not know what they really want to do other than doing what they feel they should do. Many *blocked ultra-sensitives* enjoy working more than relaxing because they know exactly what is expected of them. Many times they have to work hard at playing. They take great comfort in the safety of knowing what is expected because then they cannot do the "wrong" thing.

They are into denial when confronted with any-thing that does not fit into their belief system. Denial can come in the form of avoidance by shutting down when listening to someone telling them something. They are listening but not hearing because they have let their mind drift to something they would RATHER hear than being faced with what they do not WANT to hear. As long as life supports them in what makes them feel content for the moment, they want no more than that in their life. They do not like to think about the philosophy of life; they just want to live and be left alone. They do not want to delve into self-development until a crisis hits their life and forces them to change. As soon as they have changed as much as they feel they have to, or as much as they were forced to change by circumstances, then they go back to most or all of their old patterns. They resist change in themselves at all cost.

The talent of *blocked ultra-sensitives* is the ability to stop crisis, emotional pain, or suicide until the person in pain (which includes themselves) can find a solution or move out of the pain or crisis. That is why these ultra-sensitives can be so strong in their resistance to change. Most of the time they are using their talents AGAINST the change that is for their own good. They are the only ultra-sensitives who can stop or block time/change for the moment. *Blocked ultra-sensitives,* in their positive mode, can do this for only a very short time and only for healing of the body, mind, emotions, or spirit. They cannot use this ability for show or demonstration. It is set within them that their talent can be used only when a need arises. Remember—there is a need within them or they would not be calling on their talent or be resistant. Their talent to block a negative happening for the moment will be there to call on as long as the need for their abilities is there.

7. The Multi-talented Ultra-sensitive

If you find that you have more than one of the ultra-sensitive abilities described, it means that you are a *multi-talented ultra-sensitive* with one or more predominant types of ultra-sensitivity. Example: You may be a strong *feeling ultra-sensitive* accompanied by a touch of *knowing ultra-sensitivity.* Also at times you may have flashes of *visual ultra-sensitivity.* Then you are a *multi-talented ultra-sensitive.* This type of ultra-sensitivity can be working towards your benefit, or it can be used to create obstacles in your life.

AN AWARE, WELL-DEVELOPED MULTI-TALENTED ULTRA-SENSITIVE HAS ALL THE ULTRA-SENSITIVITY TALENTS WITH UNCONDITIONAL LOVE, POWER, AND BALANCED CONTROL

It would be a good balance for you to be able to call upon whatever ultra-sensitivity that you needed for any moment in your life. That is the ideal, and it IS possible for ultra-sensitives to call on their talents at will, and to become a positive force in the universe.

These descriptions have been designed to let you, as an ultra- sensitive, know and recognize your talents. To let you know that there are others like you experiencing the same things that you are, and that **you are not alone.**

EXERCISES

How to recognize painful patterns that repeat themselves

1. Do I make my choices without really knowing why I choose the things I do?

If you answered yes, it means you are choosing from learned patterns and not from what you really want to choose. **Trust yourself**, not the learned patterns.

2. Was my childhood painful? Does every choice I make seem to make my life more painful?

Find someone to help you who you feel you can trust. This will be the person that will help you with non-judgment. Listen to your heart about who you can really trust. Learning to listen to your heart is risking a step at a time, seeing if each step you take will hold you up. If it does, then take another step. If it does not hold you up or prove itself out, then backtrack until you find one of your decisions that WILL hold you up and prove itself out.

3. Do I know how to stop making the choices that cause me problems?

4. Who can I trust to help me?

This is the question ultra-sensitives most often ask themselves. The answer is that **you must trust yourself first**. Trust yourself to know which person or persons can help you out of your confusion. Reach out a step at a time until you know you can trust yourself to know which step is the best one to take.

3 Sources of Information

THE REASON THAT thoughts come into your mind is that you had nothing specific on your mind right then. When your mind/channel is clear or open you can and usually will *pick up* from whomever or whatever you are around. If there was a tragic accident along the road, the ultra-sensitive would *pick up* the emotions that were released by the people who had the accident, because their emotions will remain in the area of the accident long after they are gone. The fear/shock/confusion emotions remained imprinted on anything porous enough to absorb them in the area. Those emotional imprints could be read by any ultra-sensitive with the ability to *pick up* those emotions.

There are also times when you do *pick up* things because you have something very specific on your mind. What you have on your mind causes you to tap into or tune into anything that is of a "like frequency" or "like thought." You also draw information to yourself by having something very specific on your mind. When you are in **any extreme condition**, you are out of balance and become a receptor for emotional input from anyone you are connected with or anything that you are around.

Many times the way you are affected depends upon the intensity of the experience. The energy called "thoughts, feelings, or ideas" can be left in an area, in a house, in the ground, or in a person for years. At this point I am still talking only about energy and nothing else but energy. Your mind can actually *pick up* thoughts that were created and left in an area if your mind is in a quiet state or in the same frequency or state as the energy you encounter.

You can also *pick up* feelings/information/thoughts when you are feeling "disconnected" from yourself to the degree that you will start doing exactly what the person you are *picking up* from is doing or feeling. It will feel exactly like your thoughts or feelings but they will not be yours because you feel "out of sorts"— somehow you do not quite feel like yourself. Many times you will find yourself using words like these:

1. "I don't feel like myself today."
2. "I don't know what is wrong with me."
3. "I am out of sorts today."

When you use this terminology you are in fact telling yourself that you are NOT yourself. You are connected to someone else by your desire or by theirs.

You are also telling yourself that something has been *picked up* by you that is not you. (Use the "clearing tool" of saying your name; see Chapter Five.)

Another indicator to look for is that of having thoughts of a particular person come repeatedly to your mind during your day. That is also a connection. When you are doing tasks that do not take your deep concentration and the same person keeps coming into your mind, it means that you have connected with that person or that person wants to or already has connected with you. That is why s/he is on your mind or keeps coming into your mind. You may think of someone you have not seen in years, and then this person will show up. That is also your mind *communication center* working properly.

Extreme emotions stay in the area that they were imprinted or experienced in until they are consciously cleared by someone who has the knowledge and experience to clear them. In order to *pick up* traumatic emotions the *ultra-sensitive* must be any one of the following:

1.   Consciously in tune (thinking in similar ways), or
2.   low in body energy, or
3.   low in mental-emotional energy, sometimes to the point of exhaustion.

The ultra-sensitive must also have a worry or concern in the same general area in order to be open to that channel or those thought patterns.

An example: You go to visit friends after having a hard day at work and a conflict with the boss. When you arrive at your friends' house, the air feels still and electric, as if something has just happened. You may feel that maybe they did not really want to see you, or perhaps they are mad at you about something. You may even feel uncomfortable and want to leave, but you are unsure of how to do that without hurting someone's feelings. Then you find out in a few minutes that your friends have just had an argument.

Your awareness has attuned you to the circumstances that match your experience of the day/hour/moment. Your conflict with your boss attuned you to the awareness that something was wrong with your friends. You were not sure exactly what happened until they told you. Then you received verbal information that verified what your intuitive senses were giving you. If you had had a perfect day at work it would have taken more physical information to *pick up* on the same circumstances when you visited your friends.

What is meant by "more physical information" is that you would have had to notice tears, or the fact that they were not talking, or one or both of them would have had to talk to you about the fact that they were not talking. If none of this had occurred, you would not have *picked up* information about the argument.

Emotional traumatic experiences can be left in houses, in the ground, in people, in burial grounds, in sacred places, and can be experienced at any time from anyone that is ultra-sensitive enough to *pick up* the information. It does not always have to be negative emotions that are *picked up*. There are many places where positive emotional experiences are stored. Any place or area can have both positive and negative emotional experiences stored at the same place. They could have been stored there at different times in the past.

Stonehenge in England is a mysterious place where information is stored. Many different sources of information available about Stonehenge say that possibly it was used as a place to gather information about our solar system.

There is another thought that it is a place where people performed rituals to create an understanding within themselves. There are also some authors that believe that Stonehenge was used for human sacrifice.

Example: Stonehenge was visited by Alice. She loved Stonehenge and felt more alive and more certain of herself than she had in years. She felt the mystery of being at Stonehenge and felt a compulsion to sit down. Then Alice had an exciting mystical experience. She sat quietly, by what she was mentally told was the main gateway. Her "teacher" came to her and told her what they were to accomplish together. Then he touched her on the forehead as he left.

Alice now knew what her life path was and what she had come into this life to accomplish. She also knew that most of her work was ahead of her. She understood herself better and knew now why she had searched for so many years. She knew she was to have a life partner to share her life. Alice felt satisfied within herself. She felt something was complete for the first time in her life.

Alice was working with "beginnings" in her life. She found the knowledge she needed to start her new beginnings. Alice was open to new answers, and now she had to return home to implement them.

Example: The next person to experience Stonehenge was Sonja. Sonja was excited to visit a place she had always dreamed about. She felt she was to learn something about herself that she had always wanted to know. She arrived at Stonehenge and, although she felt apprehensive, she was determined to see her life's dream. When she entered the area of Stonehenge, she felt cautious and on alert. She felt directed to walk forward, and the farther she walked, the more she felt that there were other people around—although she did not see anyone physically.

Then she felt that she was witnessing a ritual of sacrifice. She felt as though she were "remembering," but that was not possible since she had not been here before. Then she felt as though she were the one being sacrificed, and she started screaming. The next thing she was aware of was someone physically standing beside her and shaking her, asking if she was okay and asking what was wrong.

Sonja had this experience because in her life at that time she was going through changes that made her feel as though she were losing everything she had used as guidelines in her life. She connected with the past life experience that showed her the ritual she had experienced in the past. The reason she was again going through the experience of giving up her life for others—

this time symbolically—was that she was saving no time for herself in her daily life.

She needed the experience in Stonehenge to remind her not to sacrifice herself any longer. Nor could she allow herself or her time to be sacrificed by others any more. She needed that experience to allow her to see what she was doing. She received this message because she was open and willing to listen. She also received the message so she could change her life. Her life was not the same from that moment on. Sonja went on to change the main relationship in her life. She also changed her career. She became visible and recognized.

4 Kinds of Intuitive Experiences

WHAT DO I DO with an intuitive experience that I do not understand? Here is a system you can use to put an intuitive experience in perspective so you can better understand what it means to you.

1. Write down your experience while it is fresh in your mind, even parts you do not understand and that do not make sense to you. Then ask yourself what happened three days prior to your experience and also what happened the day of your experience. Write it down.
2. What was happening emotionally in your life that was disturbing you?
3. Say this statement to yourself: I ACCEPT THAT MY EXPERIENCE WAS REAL AND REALLY DID HAPPEN TO ME. I TRUST MYSELF TO KNOW WHAT I FEEL/SEE/HEAR/EXPERIENCE.

4.   I accept that it was an answer to a question.
      The question that it answered was this: (Write it in
      your notebook as soon as you are aware of what it
      is.)

Step 1

Clarify the experience by writing it down or taping
it while it is fresh in your mind. Even sharing it with a
friend will help you clarify it. It will help clear it for you
so you can be more objective while processing the
information further.

When you share with a friend, be sure to choose a
friend who is understanding and open to discussing
mind-development techniques, otherwise—if this friend
is afraid or against looking at your intuitive experiences—their information will further confuse you.

Step 2

Briefly write down or tape what was happening the
day of your experience and three days prior to your
experience. This will give you correlation on why you
had the experience or what it was in reference to. As you
scan the four-day period (the day of the experience and
the three days before), record anything that you
remember about each day.

Record any emotional problems you are working
on—any people you have harmony or conflict with,
and any people you are not closely connected with but

were involved with during that four-day period of time. Record the circumstances and events no matter how insignificant or small they may seem.

Step 3

Accept that the experience was real and really did happen. Accept that you did feel or experience what you felt. Accept that you can convert it into information that will help you in some way in your life, recognizing that otherwise it would not have come to you as it happened.

Step 4

Be more understanding with yourself. Be willing to look at the fact that you accept radio and television. With television, the information travels from one station to many receivers—from seemingly nowhere. It is the same with you and the information you receive.

Your brain/mind/emotions/spirit *communication center* is a receiver that—depending on the frequency/channel/station it is set on—will receive information from many different stations, i.e. people's thoughts, words and emotions.

Which frequency/channel/station you have set your mind on depends on what is disturbing you in your emotional channel. It depends on what you are unconsciously looking for in the way of understanding or answers. It also depends upon the fact that sometimes you are not thinking or concentrating on anything, so your "computer" uses that time to answer past questions that you did not have time or energy for in the past—but there is an empty place to fill in the present.

Your *communication center* puts things on hold until there is an opportunity, time, or space available to deal with them. If something is upsetting you, that is the channel you have set your mind on and that is what you will *pick up*. You will connect with that which is most similar to what you are thinking about or are concerned about at that time. Anything that makes an emotional impact upon your consciousness will be stored, to be acted upon at a later, more opportune (sometimes inopportune!) time.

If you are afraid to fly: Maybe you have flown before, but all of a sudden you are afraid to fly. It is not "all of a sudden." Something in your life has triggered the fear; it was created to alert and protect you. Your mission is to figure out what it is, if it is appropriate, and where it came from, in order to feel safe again and know that you really are *safe* in flying. Even go to the point of creating a new structure of belief systems that will alert you if you are truly in any danger when you are flying.

Create a New Structure-of-Belief System

1. **What do I want to replace?** (old belief system).
2. **Write out your new belief system.** Make sure you use the **PAST TENSE** in your description of your new belief system.

3. **Look at your new belief system.** Is it something you would ask for, for the person you love most in your life? If not, change it. When it is good enough for someone you love, it will also be good for you.
4. **Does it feel smooth when you say it out loud?** If it does not, it is not quite right yet. Read it to someone and ask her/him to listen to how it sounds. Make necessary changes, as s/he is listening, to your new belief system.
5. **Repeat your new belief system** once a day for seven days or until it feels complete. Remember to repeat your belief system as often as you can find time, in order to establish it in your life.

What do You do if You are Receiving a Message of Danger?

1. **Honor your** *communication center* by believing **for the moment** that there is a danger. (Interpretation of "danger" may be different to your inner self than what your "conscious self" consciously believes.)
    I accept that there may be danger. (Write out your acceptance of the fact that there may be danger, but also that you can change it by knowing about it.)
2. **Look into present life experiences.** You are looking for danger in your present life. Write brief thoughts.
3. **Look into childhood experiences.** What happened? Write brief thoughts. (You are looking to see if the danger is past danger registering as present danger.)

4.   **Look into past life experiences.** What are you feeling? What culture? What is happening? Keep asking questions until you get answers. Was the danger in past lives? Is your present life triggering past fears and awakening them?

5.   **When you meet resistance or a blank wall with no feedback, then you have found what you are looking for.** Most of the time you need to look at what you would rather NOT look at. That is another way to find the information you are looking for. What do I not want to look at?

6.   a) **Talk to someone about the information you have found** until you feel complete or finished. Then and only then is it done. Who do I want to talk to about my experience?

     b) **Do you feel complete or finished with the experience? If not,** there is more information to know. What is it?

7.   **Now create what the new reaction will look like** compared to the old experience by talking about it. See yourself doing and progressing in the new experience. Describe what **your new reaction will be.**

If you have a fear of flying. This fear may come from your experience of a dear friend or family member who died in an airplane crash. It may come from a movie that you saw about flying that made an imprint on your consciousness. It may be that as a child you were waiting for someone to come to visit and s/he died in a plane crash and did not arrive. It could be that there are so many changes going on in your life that being in a plane under the pilot's control makes you feel out of control and creates overwhelming conflict for you. It could come from a past life where you were buried alive in a casket and you were drugged, completely aware of what was happening, and had no control over what was going to happen. The plane could symbolize a past life in which you had no control over a life-threatening situation. So at the present time your *communication center* is bringing you the message that there is danger of your losing control of your life, and the plane symbolically represents danger.

You may interpret it as danger in the plane. If there is physical danger in flying, the fear would not come up every time you fly. It would come up **only** on the plane trip in which there is a potential physical danger. But you must clear up all the messages of danger that do not apply to true physical danger on a plane so you CAN receive a message when it is a true physical danger.

All events in your *communication center* that have to do with flying are activated every time you fly. Some of the events may seem traumatic and some of the events you may barely remember. Some you may not remember at all and you will need someone to help you discover what they are. All these events contribute to the sum total of your knowledge of planes and flying. You may even feel responsible for a problem that happened with flying and not be aware of it consciously. Your frequency/channel/station is set to *pick up* anything to do with airplanes and flight so you will *pick up* airplane disasters before, after, or during the time they are happening.

The airplane may remind you of an event that has nothing to do with planes but triggers that memory within you that connects you to airplane accidents. It is also true that you may have had experiences (as mentioned) and you do not *pick up* on airplane disasters. The reason for this would be that you have resolved all things to do with those events in your life. Your life is reasonably stable and there are no loose ends.

If you have fear about coming events in your personal life. If you fear changes that are coming for you, you will tune into all sorts of changes: earth changes, political changes, changes in your friends' lives, changes in your company at work, etc.

The reason that you may not *pick up* or *tune in* could be that your emotional channels are already filled with other information that has a higher priority in your life at the time. There is only so much that will fit, in any given time, in your emotional/intuitive channels. This is not true of our brain/mind. Our brain/mind can store endless amounts of information and still not be filled.

There is a definite selection process determined by the needs of the individual on how the emotional/intuitive/channels are filled. That selection is made by the physical/mental/emotional/spiritual needs of the person in order of "priority survival." Priority survival is that need which is the highest priority for survival of the whole person in connection with all the systems of the individual: body, mind, emotions, and spirit.

Step 5

You can learn to control and understand exactly how your receiver works by experience. The more you work with it, the better you will understand your abilities. The more you work with your abilities, the more experience you will have. The experience that you gain will help cause the information that you receive to make more sense when you receive it. Eventually you can learn how to understand "timing" so that you will also know if the information you are receiving is about something that is happening, something that will happen, or something that has already happened.

The more you learn about yourself, the better able you will be to recognize clearly how to apply the information that you receive. **ALL THE INFORMATION THAT COMES INTO YOUR MIND IS VALID.** It is important for you to verify this in your life more and more. It is your INTERPRETATION of the information that creates the inaccuracies, and not the information itself. For instance, you may feel that the information relates to your personal life when in fact it relates to your professional life or the professional life of a friend, or even to the life of someone you are angry with. You need only an emotional tie—not necessarily a friendly emotional tie—to make an empathy connection.

Step 6

When you deny an answer to your questions your mind *communication center* has no other resource than to bring you the answer symbolically. A "symbol" is something that is used in place of something else to lead you to the information you need. Symbols are used when your mind *communication center* does not know any other way to bring you the information. Look for symbology in the information you receive. If the information you receive does not correlate exactly to your present life or circumstances, then there is symbology involved in the message. If it does not match 100% to a life experience, then there is symbology in the information you have received. Once you figure out what the symbology is, then you will see that the remainder of the information is accurate and should match a life situation exactly. A symbol is something that is used in place of something else to lead you to the information you need.

If, in a dream or vision, you see an old friend in a new situation, your old friend is a symbol of something that is old and kind to you—if in fact that old friend was kind to you in your dream. If the old friend was unkind in your waking life, then that information means something that is old in your life is coming back into your life and is NOT going to treat you kindly.

The fact that you have had a vision or a dream means that you can actually change the coming events if you want to by realizing what the old thing was in your life. If it is an old pattern, then you can change that and then the old friend (old pattern) will no longer be there to be unkind to you. That is how you can change your life. It does not matter if the information comes to you in a dream or in a vision. It would not come to you if it did not mean something to you.

It also means that you can change something in your life so that the negative event does not have to happen. When you experience a vision or dream, it is information from your *communication center* to help you in your life.

A. **Telepathy** is mentally receiving/sending information from one being to another being. This is the most common kind of information received and sent by the *communication center*, and is experienced by all three kinds of ultra-sensitives.

B. **Psychometry** is the ability to pick up information by touching a person, place, or thing.

C. **Empathy** is feeling/experiencing/knowing/seeing what the ultra-sensitive is *picking up* on the physical or mental/emotional/spiritual levels of what other people are experiencing/knowing/seeing/feeling.

Physical empathy is the ultra-sensitive *picking up* physical pain from another person or animal living in the present time or living in past memory or living in future precognitive experience.

Mental empathy is the ultra-sensitive *picking up* an attitude or judgment from another person, movie, book, dream, social or cultural belief, childhood attitude/memory, i.e. group opinion about someone, often followed by "emotional empathy."

Emotional empathy is the ultra-sensitive *picking up* the feelings of others: people who are thinking about them, people they are thinking about, people they have seen in their daily life, friends, relatives, coworkers, immediate family, loved ones at a distance, people the ultra-sensitive is in conflict with, people that have died and have left the physical plane of existence, people remembered from the present life past (such as childhood memory), past life connections that cannot be logically connected to anything of the present, often accompanied by physical sensations from others. Receptors almost always believe it is theirs because it is so real and strong.

D.   **Visions**: A vision is a visual experience of something that is about to happen, has happened, or is happening. Some visions are literal and some are symbolic.

A vision is an experience that you have when you are physically awake but your mind/emotions are in a drifting or floating state. To have a vision you must be in an "altered state." Altered states occur more often than most people believe. The first altered state of a vision is the state a person is in when s/he is daydreaming. The second stage of a vision is a feeling of disconnectedness with the sense of the physical-world reality.

Sometimes you can experience a vision physically by feeling it with your physical body sensations as if it were actually happening to the physical-body-you, and not just a mirror image actually happening to someone else. Many times visions can be experienced by feeling what the person is experiencing in your vision. Many times you can bring back the physical sensations as well as the emotional sensations with your will.

E. **Mediumship** is the awareness that someone or something outside yourself is wanting to communicate with you through you.

F. **Channeling** is spontaneously receiving information without any personal interpretation, often without even an awareness of information coming through until the thought/concept is complete. It can happen at times when there is no awareness at all of being a channel for someone else—for instance, in a meeting.

5 *How to Handle Your Sensitivity*

I WOULD LIKE to replace the word *"psychic"* with the word *"ultra-sensitive."* Being *ultra-sensitive* means deeply and lovingly caring about the world we live in and the people in that world. An ultra-sensitive is *in tune*. *In tune* means that there is an awareness of the world, which includes taking care of the people, animals, plants, earth . . . but not always themselves. Ultra-sensitives know, feel, or see that they are an integral part of all things of the earth.

As an ultra-sensitive you need to create a filtering system to help you survive in the world. A filtering system would consist of methods or techniques that filter out most of the negativity or emotional bombardment that you deal with in life until you strengthen yourself to the point where you need no protection at all. At that time you would be living in the state of unconditional love. Unconditional love is a state of being that has no judgment, no need to see things as "bad" or "good," no need to change people into being happy, no need to change people into your idea of what you think would make them happy.

This filtering system is called "intuitive self-defense." When you use this protection you are not defended against the world. You are filtering out the energies that are destructive to you at the moment, while at the same time you are building your strength to do more than just survive.

If somebody gets hurt, ultra-sensitives also experience the pain unless they protect themselves. If they are protected they can be clear and focused and can send energy that is available to them in order to help the people they want to help. Being "protected," means that you can be loving, caring, nourishing, healing and effective. One of my deepest goals in life is to be EFFECTIVE because in the past I have been ineffective when I have felt the hurt as deeply as other people have felt it. Now I can live my life being loving, open, caring, and sensitive without taking on other people's pain.

I can love people exactly where they are, whether they approve of me or not. For the moment I can feel their hurt and pain, then my being adjusts to understanding what it is without suppressing myself in any way—just by understanding that they need to be where they are until they choose to change. The moment they choose to change I will be available to help them in any constructive way I can.

Recognition/naming of
What is Happening

About eighteen years ago I awakened in the middle of the night not able to get my breath, trying to figure out what was going on. I was gasping for breath, frightened and not understanding what was happening to me. Then I lapsed into a comatose state, not wanting to respond to anyone or anything. Then—after many hours—instantly I felt full of energy. I found out later that I was experiencing a heart attack that a friend was having. At that point I did not understand what was happening to me. I was "stuck" in the experience until my friend died. **I thought it was me.** I heard one day after my experience that he had died. When I was told what happened to him, I realized that I had my *picking up* experience at the same time he was having the heart attack. I experienced his distress even to the point of having a total lack of energy and no response to my husband, children, or life, while my friend was in a coma.

I experienced the very same things he was experiencing. At the moment of his death I was filled immediately with knowledge of myself, my life, and my loved ones, and I was once again filled with the energy of a young woman, rather than that of a man in his sixties who was ill and weak.

Now when I experience anything similar, I know what is happening to me. These are the techniques that I use, which you can also use, when you are in rapport or connected in empathy to anyone:

1.   Ask these questions of yourself:
     Where is this coming from? Who is it?
2.   Listen to your thoughts. Listen by seeing/hearing
     who is on your mind or who keeps coming into
     your mind.
3.   Then make this statement out loud:
     THIS IS NOT MINE. I AM WHOLE, HEALTHY, AND
     HEALED. I AM MARCY. (Use your name.)
4.   Say your name over and over until the feeling/
     experience has stopped.
5.   Say your name with INTENT AND FEELING. **Mean**
     it. In this exercise you are using your name as a
     powerful mantra.

Use of Your Name

     Your name is the most powerful mantra you can
use. Everyone else uses your name with their belief of
who you are. When they say your name, you become for
that moment what they believe you to be, unless your
power of belief in yourself is stronger than theirs.
     I have also found that at the very time you need to
say your name the most, in order to gather yourself back
TO yourself, you will experience resistance in doing so.
The resistance comes because the person or persons
connected to you unconsciously (and sometimes consciously) will not want to let go. Use your will and
strong intent in saying your name. Your need to be
yourself must be stronger than their need to be
connected to you.

1. When saying your name, say it as if you were slip-
    ping into your body—as though you were putting
    on a pair of gloves.
2. Say your name and really believe what you are
    saying is true.
3. If you do not like your name, find another name
    that feels good to you and use that name as a
    clearing and centering tool.

The "Name Mantra" for Clearing and Protection

I am Marcy. I am only Marcy. There is no one
within or connected to me that is not Marcy. I
am totally and completely Marcy: body, mind
and spirit. I own my own universe and fill it
with being Marcy. (Use your own name in
place of mine.)

In ancient mystery schools people would be given
new names. You were told not to give others your sacred
name or to allow others to know it. Your name was
sacred. If you told someone else your name, then you
gave them control over your life. Giving someone your
sacred name meant giving them your energy. In this
lifetime it is still important to honor your name and
understand that it is the name of your body, your world,
your universe, your life. Your name is powerful for you
whether you feel powerful yet or not. It is a tool you may
have not gained the full use of yet.

The Three Jewel Protection

Visualize an emerald—hard, solid, and a beautiful rich green—deep inside your body, at the level of the solar plexus. Let it expand, still solid, until it has grown to a radius of two feet in all directions around your body. In other words, you are surrounded by a hard green emerald, four feet in diameter, anchored at your solar plexus. Visualize bringing bright sunlight with all the colors of the rainbow into the emerald, charging it with light and protective energy.

Next visualize a deep blue sapphire, faceted in all directions, hard, solid, inside your solar plexus center and expanding out until it has grown to a radius of two feet in all directions, pushing the emerald out two more feet. You are now surrounded by an emerald four feet in diameter and a sapphire two feet in diameter, both anchored securely at your solar plexus center.

Finally, visualize a hard, brilliant diamond inside your body at the solar plexus. Do not use a crystal at this point for your protection. Use a diamond when you need strong protection inside the sapphire and emerald. Start the diamond as a solid, hard, multi-faceted jewel that has all the colors of the rainbow playing within it, always moving and never still.

It has a life of its own coming from your creative force designed to protect you. Let the diamond expand until it has grown to a radius of two feet in all directions, pushing the sapphire and emerald out further.

Now you are surrounded by an emerald six feet in diameter, a sapphire four feet in diameter, and a diamond two feet in diameter, all anchored solidly deep inside your body at the solar plexus center.

Now for the final part of your protection, place in your heart's golden center an unconditional loving child that is the purest form of you to radiate out all your unconditional loving energy, to remind you to be unconditional in all your connections with all people including yourself. Now charge all your gems with more sunlight to give them life. I suggest that you use this exercise daily and on some days reinforce it as many times per day as is necessary to keep you a clear, loving, open, person that shows forth your light to the world.

6 How to Tell the Difference Between Your Personal Feeling and Your Higher Guidance

ONCE YOU ARE able to move your personal fear, guilt, or worry feelings out of the way, you will be able to see the true information that is not clouded with personal fear. It is personal fear, judgment, guilt, or worry feelings and NOT your higher guidance if ANY PART of your experience is like the following:

1. An inner rigidness to hold on to the way you see it, and a feeling of judgment of "That's just the way it is."
2. Inflexibility of fear that you will miss or lose something if you let go of any part of it.
3. Sometimes an inner unreasonableness against changing your perception.
4. An inner unspoken deeper anger that does not fit the occasion.

5.   An inner refusal, out of fear, to listen to anyone or anything else.
6.   An inner feeling of resistance against most of the information that is being presented to you.
7.   An inner stubbornness with a need to hold on to your information, accompanied by the feeling that no one really understands.

What you are experiencing is information from your higher guidance with your personal interpretation blocking the full meaning of what the complete information is telling you.

The fear that causes you to react in this way comes from the feeling that someone you love (or yourself) is going to get hurt. You want to make sure that everyone you love is going to be okay. You also want to make sure that you are going to be okay. To do this you must get your personal self out of the way. You must keep yourself clear enough to listen and hear true danger, not danger born of potential fear.

How to Receive Useful Information from My Intuitive Experience: How to Get My Fear-self, Blame-self, or Guilt-self Out of the Way

The way to use this exercise is to keep answering all the questions. Skip the questions you cannot answer. Then go back through again and answer the questions until you have an answer for all of them. Have patience wth yourself and all the answers will eventually come. The reason you ask these questions is to separate yourself personally from the experience. Use your notebook for this.

1. When did I start feeling/knowing/seeing the experience?
2. Describe what you feel/know/see in as much detail as you can.
3. Answer as many questions as you can about your feelings:
   * Are there people involved? How many?
   * When? What kind of day/night/afternoon?
   * Weather/season? What are people wearing (to help figure out the season)? Is it raining, windy, snowing, sunny? Are there leaves on the ground like autumn?
   * If there are no people, what are the area and surrounding area like?
   * What kind of time frame are you dealing with? How long before it happens? Has it already happened?
   * Is there a feeling that time is running out?
   * Is there a feeling of distance as far as miles? How far? How many miles?
   * Is it some place that you have been before?
   * What does it look like? Describe it.

Give yourself time to *feel* after asking yourself each question. If you rush through the exercises you will lose the benefit of what the questions are meant to do for you.

Important Question!

Am I seeing/feeling/knowing what is happening? or is it happening to me? Am I watching? Am I feeling as if it were me rather than its actually being me? Am I watching?

If you come up with information that is not included in the questions above, put that information down also. Keep working with the experience until you feel complete within yourself.

If you do not have a completed feeling, then you do not have all the information you need to learn from the experience. It may take you ten minutes, two or three days, or even longer to know completely what the experience means to you.

As long as you have a judgment (a one-way emotional viewpoint) about where it fits in your life, or IF it fits in your life, you are still seeing the experience from your personal prejudiced self and not receiving from your higher guidance.

You will also find that when you receive personal information it is centered in the stomach, which is an energy center underneath the rib cage. It is a nagging, persistent, muddy, all-pervasive feeling. It is often a reflection of your fears, worries, wants and judgments. When you are receiving information from this area, it comes in the form of constant emotional information that does not let up or go away unless something else in your life demands a higher priority. It always feels as though it is yours because it is all-encompassing and you feel it on all levels.

If you are a *knowing ultra-sensitive,* then you know it on all levels. If you are a *visual ultra-sensitive,* then you will see it on all levels of your life. It usually brings the feeling of "What's the use of my doing anything? My life is always going to be like this." Yet last week your life was not like this. Many things pointed to the fact that your life is changing. When we receive information only through the energy center in the stomach, many times it causes us to see only that which is happening at the time.

YOUR FEAR-SELF WILL ALWAYS SPEAK TO YOU IN EXTREMES

There is also an aggravated, restless fear—that "time-is-running out" feeling—that is a part of receiving information from your fear-self rather than your higher self. Information from your fear-self will point out the many things that can go wrong. It may also go to the other extreme of pointing out that nothing can possibly go wrong with what you want to do. In other words, your personal self will almost always speak to you in extremes. It will give you information that is not balanced and will be information that is usually all "yes" with no contradictions, or all "no" with no exceptions.

Whether you know the name of your spiritual guide or not, your higher guidance will give you information that is subtle, calm and with no sense of nagging or emotional emergency at all. Your higher guidance may give you a message of urgency but it will not have the fear attached to it that it does when it is a message from your personal fear-belief or fear-experience center. When the message from your higher self is about danger, even with a time limit, the information will be firm, direct, and clear, with a feeling of authority and calm that gives you the right information and as much room as possible to make the final decision.

YOUR HIGHER GUIDANCE WILL SPEAK TO YOU SOFTLY WITH NO JUDGMENT

At this point, ask for help from your higher guidance. Ask your higher guidance to bring the information to you in a direct, concise way that you will recognize immediately. Make a statement, either in your mind or out loud, that you are open and willing to listen to additional information about what is happening. Then be open and willing to hear whatever is given to you, whether you agree with it or not. After you receive any information, you always have the free will choice to use it as you wish or not to use it at all.

The information from your higher guidance comes to you usually in your heart-energy center. There is a quietness and stillness that accompanies it and causes you to listen even though you may not follow the information it gives you. There is a gentleness, the feeling of a guiding hand, that is giving you the option to listen or not. There is a feeling of patience and acceptance that is not stated but is usually felt and understood. The message is usually so soft that you can miss it if you do not pay attention.

It is also very easy to dismiss the message from your higher self at first because it is so gentle. Messages from your higher self are crystal clear. They are given once, then you are given time to respond. If the message is urgent, then it will be repeated as often as necessary to protect you. There is no need within your higher self to control you for any reason whatever.

Your higher self does not replace your connection with God. It is just the higher part of you that has available information that you cannot always see from your perspective. Many times in our physical daily life we get in our own way of what we want to achieve. Your higher self is there to help you overcome that.

It is true in our spiritual life that we get in the way of our connection with that higher part of ourselves. We do that by our doubt, distrust, fear, limited acceptance, or judgment that this is not the way things in our lives are supposed to happen.

The way to get in touch with your higher self is to find a quiet place where you will not be disturbed. Verbalize a prayer or affirmation to quiet your being. In your prayer ask that your personal limitations and judgments be set aside for this time. Ask to be open and willing to listen and even willing to hear something that you do not want to hear. Ask that you receive only positive information, even if it is information that is telling you about danger or something upsetting to you. Ask that you be given the tools necessary to overcome the danger or to help yourself or the person in danger.

Ask for tools to go beyond the things that are blocking you. Ask for information on how you can change the circumstances or events that you do not want to happen. Keep asking until you receive an answer you can work with or understand.

Most times people stop too soon in asking for information in connection with their higher guidance. If you receive an answer that is unclear, then ask again. If you receive an answer that is STILL unclear, ask again. Keep on asking until you have received a precise and direct answer. Remember sometimes the answer is: no answer. "No answer" is a very precise, direct answer that says everything is as it should be even though you cannot see it at the time. Sometimes "no answer" is simply a matter of timing and it is better to take no action. It means that at this time there is no answer, so wait and ask again later.

If you are not sure how long to wait, wait until you want to ask again even if it is in the next minute. You can ask as many times as you want to, and as much as you want to, until you get an answer. What you will learn is a sense of timing. Eventually you will learn to ask when the correct answer is available. If you are not sure—ask again.

When I say to ask your higher guidance, this is the procedure I recommend you use until you develop your own way of contact:

1.   Before you start, decide your purpose or reason for contacting your higher self.
2.   Find a quiet place where you will not be disturbed.
3.   Speak a positive prayer or affirmation to set a positive tone. Speak in your own words, in your own way, and with sincerity.

4. Be willing to hear your higher self through your own thoughts. Do not question what you receive until the message is complete. You give your friends the courtesy of listening without interruptions, so do the same for your higher guidance.

5. Test the information before you act upon it in your life. Give the information the test of time. See how many times the information you have received is accurate or workable in your life before you take action in your physical world.

6. Information from your higher guidance should bring balance, centeredness, trust, and a feeling of inner peace.

7. Even though you may not agree with the information from your higher guidance, or you may not want to do what it suggests, there should be an underlying feeling that applying this information in your life will create good in the long run.

7 How Judgments Affect My Life in the Here and Now

WHAT IS JUDGMENT? There are many positive parts of judgment that help us conduct our lives in a happy, balanced and useful manner. To judge means to discriminate with reason for a positive conclusion. Even with our intuition we need positive judgment to relate the information to our life. Because of the information our intuition makes us aware of in the physical world, we must weigh and balance our intuition and then take definite action.

When we create judgment in our lives, we enter into the area of *cause and effect* by putting a negative conclusion on another person, ourselves, a circumstance, or event. We can come to a conclusion about anything including ourselves, just as long as we do not say that our personal belief system (the way WE would do it or the way WE would see it) is the ONLY course of action.

NEGATIVE JUDGMENT IS A DECISION TO CREATE LIMITS FOR YOURSELF OR OTHERS

When we deliver our conclusion with a sense of "verdict" or sentencing a person to his or her ultimate doom, we create a negative karmic judgment. When you make a "that's the way it is" declaration with the personal belief that a person is wrong, this causes that judgment to come back to you. In any way that you limit any people in your perceptions of them or what they can and cannot do, you are judging them. That judgment will come back to you because the making of that judgment will create the same or similar circumstances to happen in your life as happened in the life of the person you judged. This is consistent and does not vary with the largest or smallest judgment.

Another way to understand how judgments affect your life is to look at the judgments you make about other people. Once you judge them in any way that creates an idea of limitation about or to them, you are karmically hooked into them until that judgment within you is released. Until you are willing to accept the fact that they are fine just the way they are, and you CAN understand why they are reacting as they are, the hook is still connected from you to them. You are feeding them energy on a daily basis unless you are willing to give back to them the control of their own lives, in your thoughts or in your actions.

Energy runs downhill like water. Let me give you an example. Let us say you have a friend named John. If you are the one with more energy, the energy will go to John from you. If you are the person with less energy, then the energy will run from John to you. Throughout the day there may be a tradeoff of energy unless John is going through an emotional upheaval. It is highly likely in that case that you will be supplying energy for John. Until you are willing to accept the fact that John is strong enough to handle his own life, whether you APPROVE of the way he handles it or not, you will be an energy resource for him any time that he needs to tap your energy for himself.

John does not even have to reach out consciously to tap into your energy supply because when you judged him you gave him an open line to your energy whenever a need within him arose. He is not draining you on purpose. He knows instinctively where energy is available and his survival system is using the line you created (with your judgment) as a connection to you— and your energy. Once you judge a person you automatically give that person permission to tap your energy day or night.

A judgment is a limited belief about someone. It is being conditional about someone, being non-accepting of a person, her/his conditions or actions. Usually with people we love, we have fear for their well-being so we try to help them. In our wanting to help, many times we end up limiting them by pointing out the problems or obstacles to the point where we have given them no room to move. In our need to protect them we have pointed out so many obstacles that they feel weighed down by the obstacles and they become "stuck."

Contrary to what we wanted to accomplish, we accomplished the reverse. In wanting to protect them, we created a fear of doing (in them) because we emphasized all the difficult things they are facing. When we want to help those we love, it is helpful to bring them information only in connection with what they are dealing with at the present time, and not to overload them with obstacles they may have to face. Help them to create a plan to work by, so they can see what they are facing without over-emphasizing all the possible dangers.

POSITIVE JUDGMENT MEANS TO DISCRIMINATE WITH EMOTION AND REASON FOR A POSITIVE CONCLUSION

If people are looking to you for information or guidance, this means that they see you as a specialist for them in that particular area of their life. It means that you have the power to stifle or suffocate them before they even get started. You can block them from doing what they want to do simply by putting a dampening effect on their efforts, and pointing out all the obstacles they may or may not have to face. It is much like teaching a child to walk.

People will start to believe that they cannot walk without your help if you watch over them all the time and do not let them fall. They will cry and reach out to you for support. They will not want to leave your side. They will feel in danger if you are not around. They will not have learned how to stand on their own two feet. If you overprotect people to the point that your actions are telling them that you are afraid for them to be on their own, you are not strengthening them, you are weakening them.

They will be afraid of doing anything on their own. They will always come to you when they need help or direction. They will not believe that they can do it on their own without you. Support the people you love by believing in them with your words, your actions, and your thoughts. Let them fall or be in pain. Love them enough to let them bring themselves out of their difficulties. Be their strength by feeling strong about them even when they do not feel strong about themselves. Stand by to help them by backing up their belief in THEMSELVES, not their belief in their FEARS.

When people are in pain or difficulty and you do not let them handle the difficulty themselves, you are judging them in what I call a "positive-negative judgment." A "positive-negative judgment" is seeing people in pain and wanting to help them or do it for them. We believe positively that they should not be suffering in the way they are suffering. We believe that we should take the burden and carry it for them.

IN ORDER TO CHANGE ANYONE ELSE, WE MUST FIRST CHANGE OURSELVES

When we believe that other people should not be in pain, that is a personal judgment by us. What we are saying to them is that we feel that we can handle their problems better than they can. We are telling them with our actions that we believe that they are too weak to be effective. We are also telling them that they are going about the solution all wrong. We are showing them our fear: We believe that they are too weak to achieve their end result. We are saying they need to be bailed out by us.

We believe that we should do the task for them. As ultra-sensitives, when other people are in pain, we also hurt. Our solution is to help them out of pain so WE feel better. We must learn that in order to help other people out of their pain we must let them be strong for themselves. As ultra-sensitives we are famous for helping everyone else BUT ourselves. In order to change the world, we must first change ourselves.

When we take on other people's battles, we are actually taking away what they have done so far, and they have to start all over again. If they have built up to a crisis point that will cause them to change a part of their life, when we take away the crisis we are limiting them from completing what they are working on. They must begin again to build that energy to reach the same point they were at before we came along.

Many times we ask other people, "Why doesn't Sandra let me help her?" My answer to that question is that Sandra wants to get past her obstacle this time for good. If she lets someone else do it for her, she will just have to create it again in order to accomplish it and go beyond it.

There is a part of all of us that wants to help. There is also a part of us that believes that we want someone to do it for us. There is also a part of us that knows that this is not the way life works. The only way I know of to create real life changes is to "do it yourself." It is important to have supportive people around you that create a safe environment to risk your new beginnings, but the beginnings must come from within you with

the help of your God-Self. When we judge people and
their approaches to life, we are not only limiting
THEM—we are limiting OURSELVES.

There is the mother in all of us—both male and
female—that wants to nurture and nourish others. We
must approach that mother part of us with a wholistic
nature so it does not stifle the people around us whom
we love. A mother has to make judgments in order to
keep her children safe. While the child is growing up, a
mother has to make judgments even against the wishes
of the child she wants to help.

After children start to grow up and need to make
some of those decisions on their own, the mother in us
does not want to let go for fear the child will get hurt.
But if the child gets hurt in small ways that are not life-
threatening, s/he will learn how to create a powerful,
deciding, happy self. When we do not let the children
(or other people we love) decide, then our controlling
judgments are weakening them, not strengthening
them.

8 Why Bother With Past Life Information

PAST LIFE INFORMATION can be helpful to aid you in understanding what is happening in your present life. History repeats itself. If we have completed what we needed to complete in the past, then those same lessons we learned do not present themselves in this life as something we need to learn. In other words, the things we have completed do not have to be redone. If we have not completed relationships, family ties, connections or personality traits, then they are before us to do.

One way to discover what your past lives were is to look at what you like and what you cannot stand. What era of history fascinates you? What kind of clothes from the past do you just love? Where would you like to travel to in the world? What parts of past history do you feel were awful? What areas do you have no interest in at all? The knowledge of past life information is within you. It is as close as your thoughts. It does not take a great deal of concentration to bring that information forward. You carry your past life information with you all the time. The Akashic Records are your soul memory. It takes only your recognition to make them useful information to you.

You are living with your past life information in your life right now. What kind of furniture do you have in your house? Does your house have the flavor of another country or past history? Are you an antique collector or would you be if you had extra money? Do you not want antiques around but rather modern furniture? How do you feel about food?

I have a friend named Doreen who likes to have her cupboards full at all times. When you go to Doreen's house she always welcomes you by wanting to know if you have eaten yet. She is a beautiful and gracious hostess that makes anyone in her home feel welcome. Doreen feels that she has treated you badly if you do not have the opportunity to have something to eat when you visit her. Doreen loves Chinese furniture, and the vases and ornaments she has in her home have Chinese decorations on them. Some of Doreen's happy past lives of affluence and enough food for herself and her family were in China. That is the reason in the present she loves Chinese decorations.

She is a loving and caring person who wants to make sure you are comfortable. Her past lives are showing through in the way she treats the people she cares about who come to visit her. Doreen had starved to death in several past lives. Food is very important to her because she had to watch her children starve to death a little every day. She cannot stand to think that someone—or even her animals—would be hungry. Her soul memory reminds her that starving is a painful death.

If you have not completed a past life tie with a person in a past life, then you will be back with that person in this life . . . or a similar person. In this life the situations will be the same as in the past life, unless you have already learned the lessons that were there for you. If you HAVE learned the lessons, then both of you can create new, happy, and successful connections with one another. I know of two people in this life who had been together in ten past lifetimes.

Each time they were together they could not decide whether they should get married or not. In the past, each time the wedding date got close, one or the other of them left the town or the country. No matter which one was the male, he left before they faced a permanent relationship together. In this life they were living together and kept thinking of getting married. They did not understand what was stopping them until they learned of their past lives. In this life, they would get close to marriage and one or the other would want to run for no apparent reason, and yet they were both sure they loved one another.

Once they learned of their past lives and of how they avoided a commitment to each other, they talked it out together and decided that there was no present life reason for stopping the marriage. They were married and are having fun creating their life from this point on instead of remaining stuck in the past. Once you understand the pattern from the past, then you can use your reasoning abilities in the present life to help you go beyond what is stopping you, especially when it does not seem to have a concrete reason for being there in this life.

Many times people will ask me, "What if past life information is not real and is just our 'cellular' ancestral memory?" I tell them that although past life information is very real, it does not matter whether it is past life information or gene and ancestral knowledge that is blocking or stopping you. It does not matter whether it is a negative past life or a rebellious ancestor that you are carting around as excess baggage. It is just important to get the block out of the way and get on with living a full, rich, and rewarding life.

I work hard not to get stuck in the technicality of words when I am interested in getting movement in my life or in the life of anyone I am working with. Words are a very important tool, but they are useful only if I do not use them to block myself by getting stuck in the terminology as an excuse not to create movement in my life.

How do I know that past life information is true? You can tell if past life information is true by how you respond to it. If it is true there will be an "Ah ha!" when the information is presented to you. There will also be a feeling of clarity—that of "So that's why I feel as I do." You should get some sense of completion from receiving information and answers about past lives.

9 How Do You Change the Things You Want to Change in Your Life?

I WOULD LIKE to help you understand that you are exactly as you are supposed to be. Yes, I know there are many things about yourself that you would like to change. But even though you do not fit into other people's ideas of what they think you should be, or even your own idea of what you think you should be, that does not mean that you cannot change the things about yourself that you would like to change.

It means that you should keep those things about yourself that are good, kind, and thoughtful of all life. It does not mean you cannot change. It just means "self-acceptance" for and in the moment. You are exactly as you should be. There is an explanation for every experience that you are having. If you will remember to ask for an answer, you will receive it.

ACCEPT YOURSELF IN THIS MOMENT. GIVE YOURSELF THE RIGHT TO CHANGE IN THE NEXT MOMENT.

There is also something you can do right at this moment to help yourself and still retain your own individuality. The following steps are designed to help you through experiences that you find yourself in whether or not you know why they happened or how you got there.

1. It is important for you to understand that what-ever comes into your mind is there for a purpose or it would not be there.

2. The way to solve the problem or just make it go away is—first, accept that it is there.

3. The experience you are having is filled with infor-mation of something that you are involved in. It means something to you or it would not be happening to you.

4. When you are having an experience that you can-not explain, all the information that you need to understand it is within you at that moment. Find a quiet place. Ask out loud. Be willing to listen to the things you do not want to hear. It is just that you are so used to seeing the problem, that you cannot see the solution.

In the beginning you must bypass your logical mind in order to search for the answers. When you find the answers, they will fit into a logical and reasonable sequence explaining why you had the experience. Only when you have arrived at the final answer for that experience will that be true.

It has been proven to me over and over that everything that comes into your mind is valid. The information that you are receiving means that your *communication center* is working even if your logical mind cannot fit the information into its well-ordered universe.

If the information we receive does not fit into what is happening in our lives at a time when we are looking for specific information that we feel will resolve a problem, we toss out all the information that we feel does not apply, and consider it erroneous. Many times you ask for information, then forget that you asked for it. When the answer does arrive, you throw it out because you do not remember having asked the question!

For instance: My mother died when I was five months old. From the time I was very young I had always wanted to know what my mother was like. So, at the age of thirty, I started asking in my thoughts and prayers to know what my mother was really like. About two months later I started having Taurus women coming into my life who wanted to take care of me. They were loving, beautiful women who had lost someone in their lives. Even though I appreciated their caring, I also felt frustrated at not being able to do things for myself that I needed to learn. I forgot that I had asked that I wanted to know my mother.

Then in my meditation I got the answer to both my questions: "What was my mother like?" and "Why are

---

WHEN YOU ASK A QUESTION, YOU WILL
ALWAYS GET AN ANSWER

---

all these Taurus women coming into my life?" I thanked the universe for giving me the information that I had asked for and I also asked that my "mother images" be allowed to find someone that needed their loving energy more than I did at that time. The two women that stayed in my life had something to work on together as well as something to work on with me. It is true that life is a balance, if we will truly look and see. When you ask a question, you will always get an answer.

When you ask a question of your Higher Self it is important that you write it down so you remember what you have asked. In that way you will know it when you receive it, or at the very least, you can check to see what you have asked of your Higher Self/Universal Self.

What we receive is never the wrong thing. It is our interpretation of how it fits into our lives or if it fits into our lives that may make it APPEAR wrong. Nothing comes to us unless it is FOR US.

How to Recognize Incoming Information into Your Communication Center

1. Look at *how* it comes into your communication center.
2. Pay attention to *when* it comes into your communication center.

3. Does it come *in sequence*? Know that information does not always come in 1-2-3-4 order. Sometimes 4 comes before 3, or 2 before 1. Everything that comes into your mind is valid, even if it is not in order.

An example of incoming information within a six-hour period of time:

1. While watching a fantasy movie you asked a question—thinking out loud—about how this kind of movie was made. You asked it out loud when others were around, but not directly to them.
2. You asked a question wondering how your friend Judy was. You asked this in your own thoughts.
3. You asked a question about one of your personality traits. You asked this out loud to yourself with no one else around.

I will show you how the answers to these questions could have come to you. The answers may be recognized by you and they may not be. In the following example, during the next six-hour period of time, you are also occupied with visiting a friend you have not seen in a very long time.

The first answer was to the question you asked about how your friend was doing. As you are talking to your friend you say, "Remember Judy? I haven't seen her in a long time." Then your friend says, "I saw her just yesterday. She is remarried and doing just great. She has a new baby." Then the two of you go on visiting together without either one of you realizing that the question you had asked earlier was answered. You had not even realized that your *communication center* was working perfectly and that you have just received one of your answers.

Then your friend says, "I have been wanting to talk to you about something for a long time and I haven't been sure how or where to start." Then she proceeds to tell you how she has always appreciated a specific personality trait of yours, or relates to a personality trait of yours that she has always had a hard time with.

You still may not realize it, but that is the answer to your question number three. You probably still do not remember that you asked the question or recognize that you have received the answer. Many times you will respond by saying, "That's strange. I was just thinking about that this morning before you called." Your answer to the fantasy movie may not show up for days or weeks, but it will be answered. It may come to you through a special on television telling how fantasy movies are made; it may come to you in an article in a newspaper that someone left on a seat on the bus next to you. It can come in any of a number of ways. Ask and you will receive. Your questions will always be answered—not always when you THINK they should, but they WILL be answered.

Many times when information comes into our minds we interpret it in the wrong context or we ignore it. Quite often the information creates so much fear that we, as ultra-sensitives, run away from the information we are receiving because we are afraid it will be bad news. We are afraid that it will make others feel that we are losing our sanity. Since there have been times of our OWN self-doubt, our fear doubles when we hear it from others. It is important for us to look at it thoroughly and put it into context with our life.

All information that comes into our brain/mind/ emotions/spirit *communication center* will benefit us and those we wish to support in our life. Our brain is the physical container for our mind. Our mind is the information or energy that is called "us" by our name. Another way to say this is that our brain is the "physical world part" and our mind is the "spiritual world part" of our being. They are designed to work together.

10 How You Can Find Your Special Intuitive Gifts or Talents

ONE OF THE BEST WAYS to look for your talent is to look at the very things that seem to be going wrong consistently. For instance, "Everyone is always taking advantage of me;" or "I'm always so thoughtful with everyone else and yet most people are not thoughtful with me;" or "No one really listens to me;" or "I'm more comfortable in giving than receiving."

Once you find one of these patterns, you are on your way to understanding truly how to change something about yourself that will change your life in a very powerful way. These patterns are a signal to you that your actions are affecting your life in a very definite way. Maybe not as you would like, but they ARE affecting your life.

Ginger R. kept attracting people into her life that needed help with their careers. Every time Ginger put all her effort behind them, they would succeed, but

Ginger herself never seemed to get going. She could not find what she wanted to do. She could do so many things that she was not sure what to pick as a career. She always had so much to do for others that *her* things just did not seem to get done. I spoke with Ginger about her talents and she said that she did not know what they were.

When we looked at her life, we saw that the main theme was people involved in Ginger's life. When people were in the process of working out their problems, they were always attracted to Ginger. They received help and Ginger felt fulfilled, but she also felt frustrated because it did not seem to get her any closer to a solution for a career for HERSELF. Ginger is a "people person" who needs to be in a career in which part of her job is working with people.

No matter what she did, Ginger attracted people into her life. The solution was to help her find a career that used her talents at being a success in helping people. Ginger started a job in a car rental agency, and put the energy into HER life that she had been putting into other people's lives. She acknowledged her gift with people and made it work for her. Ginger is now a successful Executive Director of Sales in a national car rental agency. She made a powerful change for herself and became a valuable asset to her company as well.

Ginger's experience is not the exception in the lives of ultra-sensitives. Her experience is more often the rule. Ginger is not stopping at this success. She is continuing her personal development in all areas of her life. By her example, she is teaching all ultra-sensitives how powerful they are in finding their place in the world.

That which seems to be a weakness that causes problems in your life is truly your strength waiting to be discovered by you. As a natural ultra-sensitive, you have the ability to "read" people on more than one level. In your childhood when you "read" a situation correctly, it was most likely so accurate that you upset the adults around you. They denied that any part of it was right. They may have simply dismissed you and told you to go out and play. They may have used statements like these: "Don't be silly. Everything is just fine!" or, "I don't have time right now." Most of the time that translated to you, the ultra-sensitive, that what you received as your inner messages were wrong and not acceptable to the people you loved.

This can cause you to doubt and not to trust yourself and your thoughts, feelings and ideas. This also may cause you, as an ultra-sensitive, to feel the need to look to others for answers because your answers did not work for you. The mixed messages occur when people are telling you one thing with their words, and their feelings are relaying a totally different message. Then they go on to repeat the very things that you said to them, to someone else. But now, because THEY said it, they are reacting as if it is totally right. When YOU said it, you were told you were wrong. This makes ultra-sensitives doubt or distrust themselves at a very early age. The messages ultra-sensitives receive is that when THEY do something it is wrong; yet when someone ELSE does the very same thing, the other person is right.

Many times when ultra-sensitives DO respond to the feeling/messages inside themselves, they can lose friendships, or create anger in family members through lack of understanding. They can even lose career opportunities because their need to verify their inner feelings is so clear and comes through so strongly. It feels to the ultra-sensitive that s/he has to prove that this clear inner message is true, or else it proves that s/he has lost touch with reality.

For ultra-sensitives, it becomes a desperate need to understand the information that comes to them. It is a matter of their survival. By listening to the feeling-messages and recording them in a journal, you, as an ultra-sensitive, can validate and clarify your feelings and know for sure that they are true.

Be sure to date the entries in your journal and correlate them with your feelings about the events or persons because this is the way you can connect this information with the physical-world-reality. Again it is STRUCTURE that will help you understand your feeling/sensory world and help you relate it to the practical world.

LEARN THAT YOUR UNBALANCED ULTRA-SENSITIVITY IS SIMPLY UNMOLDED CLAY THAT CAN BE MOLDED BY YOU INTO A BEAUTIFUL WORK OF ART

In your journal also write the person's name and connection to you as well as the brief circumstances around the events you are writing about. Then you will want to leave a space for later comments in order to verify or interpret the information you received—for your better understanding when you receive more information next time.

It is important for you to build a STRUCTURE OF PROOF that helps you understand your *communication center* brain/mind/emotions. Learn to trust your ultra-sensitivity. Learn that your unbalanced ultra-sensitivity is simply unmolded clay that can be molded by you into a beautiful work of art. You are the only one that can sculpt yourself into your balanced, creative self, with the help of YOUR INDWELLING DIVINE UNIVERSAL SELF.

Where you are right now, or how you got here, or how you are right now, is NOT WRONG. It is simply a place for you to begin, in order to get where you are going. It is like traveling, beginning in New York with your destination being San Francisco. Where you are is only where you are right now. You can change that at any time, including the very next moment.

**THERE IS NO "BAD" OR "GOOD." IT JUST IS
THE WAY IT IS UNTIL YOU CHANGE IT.**

There is no "bad" or "good." It just is the way it is until you change it. The concept of " bad" or "good" comes from your judgment or acceptance of judgment from others. It may be your own judgment of yourself or it may be someone else's judgment, but that does not make it right or wrong. It is only how you APPLY the information you receive to your life that makes it work for you or not work for you.

Success is simply continuing to do something until it works. So-called "failure" is only stopping before you reach success. If something is not working, all you need to do is to change your approach or your application of information to change the experience. If YOU do not form the experience or if YOU do not create it, there is no magic genie that is going to appear out of nowhere and form it or create it for you.

SUCCESS IS SIMPLY CONTINUING TO DO SOMETHING UNTIL IT WORKS

What you have and how you look at things and how you do things—that is your talent and gift. Because this uniqueness is your gift, it is natural for you to create it into the powerful loving tool that you are. You may not as yet have put all the pieces of the puzzle together in the total picture that is you, but this is because learning to trust yourself is a step-by-step process that is difficult in the beginning.

If you are working to start to build that trust, be as loving and kind to yourself as you are to others. Give yourself the right to miss the mark or target in reaching for your goals. Trust yourself to know instinctively when to go forward. By taking action, build the trust in yourself that was undermined by circumstances, people, and events in your life.

The natural order of nature is that all things must change, yet the learned reaction of ultra-sensitives is to want everything to stop, and if does not stop of its own accord, they try to stop it because they are afraid. It is also important to understand that sometimes "taking action" means to stop some things that you are doing. The decision not to take action at that designated period of time is still considered an action. That is entirely different from trying to make everything stop.

When an ultra-sensitive tries to stop, everything seems to fall in on her/him. To keep moving is the less painful choice for an ultra-sensitive, though it may not seem to be true at the time. Viewing it with hindsight, however, it seems always to be true. Everything seems to get worse—not better—as the ultra-sensitive works to find a place to stand still.

The key that will work in this circumstance is for you to be willing to change by going beyond old thinking patterns of "This is the way it is," or "I can't change it." Do not stand still. If you find yourself standing still, do something quickly. Take some action that will change something in your life before something out of your control moves you in a direction or in a way that you do not want to be moved. In other words, do not wait for a crisis to move you.

There is only one safe place to be still in the midst of changes, and that is within you—a place that you self-create where your philosophy or beliefs sustain you. The safest place for you is owning all that you are and expanding into that knowledge. Move with time and events and claim your place in the world. Know that the loving, ultra-sensitive being that you are is needed on this earth now more than ever. Take your rightful place by being exactly who you really want to be and as the total individual that you are.

Know that there are many things that you can do and accomplish to help yourself as well as to make an important difference in the world. It all starts, not with changing the world, but with changing yourself. But of

IT ALL STARTS NOT WITH CHANGING THE WORLD, BUT WITH CHANGING YOURSELF

course that is the best way to change the world. Change YOUR world first. Change yourself. Change the actions, change the thoughts, emotions, and thinking patterns in your life that are causing you difficulties. Take one step at a time. Change one pattern at a time, either a thought or physical action pattern. It does not matter where you start; it matters only that you do start.

If all your patterns seem important, then choose just one to start with, then proceed to the next one. You can also choose to change something you are "stuck" in in your life right at this moment. For instance, if you are having difficulty with money, start thinking about changing your thinking about money. Stop the thinking process the moment you are aware of thinking about anything that is connected with the idea that there is not enough money.

You must not play at it or pretend or just give it a try; you must live it as if it were so. You must put all your INTENT into it. When you were a child and it was three days before Christmas, how much did you want Christmas to be here so you could open your presents? Now THAT is intent! You must take charge of yourself with that kind of intent and insist and persist in getting rid of that one negative thinking pattern until it has no room to live within your life, your body, your emotions or your world.

Training your mind is like training a unique, priceless animal. Imagine yourself training the beautiful, loving, sweet dog that you fell in love with and just had to have. You paid over $1500 for your pet. When you brought the purebred home you found that it was stubborn and resistant to training. This did not stop you. You continued the training, knowing that the time you spent was going to be worth it in the end.

GIVE YOURSELF THE RIGHT TO BE WORTH YOUR TIME

It is important to give YOURSELF the same right to be worth it and to spend a great deal of time, effort and energy to succeed. Then you will be as pleased with yourself as you were in training that beautiful animal with love and kindness. Give yourself as much love and patience as you are willing to give to anyone or anything else on this earth. The animal was worth it and so are you. In training the animal you did not give in to a pattern that was harmful to the animal just because the animal persisted in responding against the new training. You invested a great deal of money, time and effort in this animal. You valued the animal enough not to give up. In that same way, you must value yourself enough not to give up.

Because your mind is not used to training, it wants to do something other than what you want it to do. If it were a computer (and it is the most unique computer on the face of this earth), you would just reprogram and work with it no matter how many bugs you had to work out. Give yourself that same kind of patience. As an ultra-sensitive, it is vital not to allow your emotional thinking processes to control you.

Self-Training Guidelines

1. I will see the value of myself.
2. I will give myself the same time to learn that I would give anyone else to learn.
3. I will be loving and patient with myself.
4. I am in training to change my life.
5. I will take one step at a time toward changing my life.
6. I will love myself in my successes AND in my failures towards my goals.

If you are thinking you may not have enough money to last through the end of the month, that may in fact be a material truth in your world. But to create more for the month you are living in, and for future months, you must start right now to change that by changing your thought processes and your emotions by stopping any emotional system in your mind as well as in the words that you are thinking or speaking, that says you do not have enough money.

If you are thinking positively, but behind that thinking you are feeling, "It is empty, hollow and useless to think you have money when you don't," if you feel you are just lying to yourself, then your emotional feelings are still overriding your conscious effort to create money. You must change your emotional feelings at the time when everything in the material wold is telling you that you are behind with your money and everything is going wrong.

I AM IN TRAINING TO CHANGE MY LIFE

I say to ultra-sensitives, "You must live in the moment. But you must not believe that what is happening in that moment will stay the same forever." What I mean by this is that you must be conscious in the physical world and relate to the physical world by living within your budget even if there is not enough money to go around, while at the same time keeping your mind focused on the new thought pattern even if it is not true at the very time you think it. Work to live within the accepted laws to the best of your ability.

You must stop yourself from believing that this moment is the way it is always going to be. Ultra-sensitives have a strong tendency to believe that what is happening to them in the moment is the way things are going to stay from that moment on.

ALL THINGS CHANGE. THIS ALSO WILL CHANGE.

That is what creates the helpless feeling in ultra-sensitives that it is useless to struggle. *At the very moment they feel that this is hopeless, it is more important than at any other time for them to fight against giving in to what is happening . . . fight the feeling belief that this is the way life is going to be from now on. Fight the belief that the negative event that is happening is true and has always been true.*

START RIGHT NOW IN ONE SMALL WAY TO CHANGE YOUR LIFE FOR THE BETTER

The way to change your life with relationships, with money, with spiritual development, with life-long blocks—is to start right now in one small way to change your life for the better. When I say "better" I do not mean OTHER PEOPLE'S idea of better but YOUR idea of better. If you believe that your money is not working and enough is not coming in, then you are creating and setting the stage for tomorrow to be the very same way, and for it not to change. What you think, act, feel and believe NOW is creating tomorrow and next week and next year.

WHAT YOU THINK, ACT, FEEL AND BELIEVE NOW IS CREATING TOMORROW

You are creating your life by your approach to life, by the way you feel about life, by the way you act, interact and react to life. If you want to change your life, then change your thoughts to the very best of your present ability.

OUR MIND IS DESIGNED TO HELP US CHANGE

Be satisfied with what you are doing, knowing it is the best you can do right now. Work to do even better tomorrow. Many ultra-sensitives tell me that they cannot help how they feel. We have been trained to believe that we feel what we feel and we cannot change our feelings, when in fact we CAN change our feelings to create happiness. Many of the patterns that we believe to be ours have been programmed into us, by our perception of events, and by society, parents, peers and people around us, and even ourselves.

Our mind is designed to help us change. If we leave that creation to others by their influence or our own influence of old patterns, then we will stay "stuck." We can continue to live our life by the belief system in us that has been created by others or events and circumstances around us, or we have the choice to go beyond being the victim and re-create ourselves in a way that works to bring us a balanced, healthy, happy life. Then—with the help of our Universal Self—we become a healthy active creation of ourselves.

OUR EMOTIONS ARE DESIGNED TO GIVE US CREATIVE OPTIONS

Taking charge of our life is not a guarantee that everything will go right. Many times ultra-sensitives will say, "I tried that and it didn't work." Of course it did not work, and there will be many times when it will not work, but there will be many more times that it WILL work. If you are keeping score on the many times that it did NOT work, then you will miss all the times that it DID work. This awareness will bring you a very real sense of who you are. After each success you will build your new foundation. After each so-called failure you will build a new understanding of what you do not want and what will not work for you.

IT IS OUR FEARS THAT CAUSE US TO STOP AND CREATE PAIN IN OUR LIFE

Ultra-sensitives usually believe that if they change their lives by working with a new system, and that new system fails to be perfect in any way, then they believe it would have not worked ANYWAY, which tells them that the whole system does not work. Instead of looking at the WHOLE SYSTEM as not working, it is important for ultra-sensitives to take out only the part that does not work for them, then work again at making it all work together.

You are the only one that can create the changes in your life that will be permanent and make you happy. Yes, there is such a thing as happiness. Happiness is the state of being where you are achieving up to your total potential, even if no one else sees that.

TAKING CHARGE OF OUR LIFE IS NOT A GUARANTEE THAT EVERYTHING WILL GO RIGHT

Even when you make a painful discovery, you can have happiness. This discovery can be the key that will unlock many blocked doors. Once you have opened these doors, you will not have to travel through that painful experience again. Happiness is the state of being all you can be, and not what you think other people think you should be. Not even what you think you ultimately should be. You can be happy in the midst of change even though you may have some fear about the change. It is a process that demands your constant openness and willingness to change without thinking about stopping—not even thinking about or wanting to find a place in the future to stop, or looking to arrive at that perfect place that you will not have to change ever again. To think that way is a trap. It will stop you from living in the moment and enjoying life. Self-change will give you more fulfillment than any other process will.

Creating changes becomes a way of life that will demand that you not go back to your old ways, even for a day, once you are awakened to this new process. Even if you do try out your old ways, you will find that they no longer work for you.

Once you have this knowledge and have applied it, then you are responsible for the knowledge. **You cannot go back to the point when you did not know.** You cannot fall asleep again and pretend that you do not have that knowledge.

That part of you that has been awakened will demand of you that you use this new knowledge in your life by showing you that the old way no longer works for you no matter how easily you think you can go back into old habits. That is how the saying, "You can never go home again," could apply.

Once you have learned beyond a certain point, you can go through the motions of the old ways, but they will no longer work for you. You will be forced to take up the new "tools," the new knowledge, and go forth into your life. You can turn aside from this new knowledge, but something inside you will force you to seek it out again and again until you own it and make it work for you.

WHAT YOU FEEL IS NOT EVER WRONG

If what you want to happen in your life is not happening, you can blame your academic or spiritual teacher, you can blame circumstances or events, you can say something is wrong for you and, if it feels wrong for you, then it will be truly wrong for you. Remember, your feelings are not ever wrong, but how you apply them in your life may not work for you. What you feel is **NOT EVER WRONG.** If what you are doing in your life feels wrong, then believe your feelings because it means that there is something wrong about something you are doing or it would not feel wrong. If it feels wrong then for you it **IS** wrong. When this happens, you have to make some choices. Change yourself and it may still be wrong; change what feels wrong, change the training, change the teacher, change your career and then it may feel right. You may go back to something that felt wrong in the past, but the timing may be right now in the present and it will be right for you.

The same thing applies if what you are doing feels right but it is not working out as you think it should. Your feelings are not wrong. If it feels right, then it is right regardless of the appearance of what is happening at the moment. Believe in your clear true feelings. If your feelings are not clear, then wait for more information or seek out more information to help you decide. If it is something that you are trying to convince yourself is right, but it does not feel right, then it is not right. If you are unclear, then do not make a choice until you have clear feelings or have received information from someone whose thoughts, ideas and decisions you would trust . . . someone who is successful in her/his life in the same area that you are working on to change your life for the better.

Remember that nothing is permanent. It is a universal truth that everything changes. If you will look around you at life, you will see the changing seasons, the changing of the animals, the changing of the people around you. Also the way all life is being lived is in constant flux and change. We are a reflection of all things that are in our world. If all things around us are changing, then we too are changing, whether we see those changes or not. On a daily basis we do not see summer changing into fall, and yet each and every day it is changing to fall; then fall is changing to winter. If we compare two months that have passed, then we can see the changes, but if we look for the changes on a daily basis we see only that day. It is true of our life also. We are constantly changing even when we do not see any changes within us at all. Once you open a door to a new truth, that door can no longer be closed to you. **Once you know something, you will be responsible for that information from that moment on.** Even if you consciously choose to forget information that you have learned, you are still universally responsible for that information. That knowledge is always yours from the moment that you know it. No one including yourself can stop you from knowing that you have that specific knowledge. If you ask for that information, it shall be given to you. Ask and you shall receive. Knock and the door shall be opened to you.

PAYING ATTENTION
TAKES PRACTICE AND OPENNESS

The best place to start looking at overcoming fears is to look for fears that you are afraid you cannot overcome. Fears are walls that are hiding who you are from yourself. Take one wall at a time and knock it down. Find a "support system" that will help you challenge your fears—someone who will listen with equal kindness to your falling short as well as your achieving; someone who will understand and always support you to go forward at your own pace and timing. **You are important to this world.** Everything in this world proves that to you, if you will listen. Every blade of grass, every animal is a part of this world and important to the sum total of the world.

It is important for you to understand that the world would be totally different if you were not here. How you live your life and how you interact with others affects everyone on this planet. There are no innocent bystanders; there are only participants in this world. Even if you choose not to participate, you are still taking an action to be in this world. Even if you choose to be a hermit on a hillside, that decision would affect everyone on this earth. No matter how you have chosen, all lives are affected just from your being here.

There is no one on this earth who could be a hero in the exact way that you could be a hero. There is no one on this earth who could be important in the same way that you are important, just by being on this earth and affecting all the people you affect in your life. If you think you do not have touch with many people, think about the grocery clerk, paper person, cleaners, bank clerk, hardware store clerk, video store person. Think of the people you make contact with when you walk down the sidewalk, read the paper, watch television. Think of the people you related to if you have had any house repairs done (or have done them yourself), or even when you drive in your car or talk on the phone. Those are only some of the people you make touch with all the time.

HOW MANY PEOPLE DO YOU MAKE CONTACT WITH WHEN YOU LEAVE YOUR HOUSE?

As an exercise, the next time you leave your house, use your notebook to name or describe all the neighbors, strangers, and friends you see for that entire day. For example: Lady crossing the street with red shoes. Man that smiled when he walked around the corner. Angry child in store with plaid shirt. Penny's husband. Lady checker at grocery store. Lady with black hat in restaurant. Lady driving white Corvette. Red-haired man changing lanes in front of me.

1. How many neighbors, strangers, and friends did you see? Describe them briefly. If you cannot remember them, then you did not connect. If you do remember them, it means that they connected with you or you connected with them. No matter how briefly you connected with them, or they with you, there is an energy drain from one of you.

Energy always flows out from the person with more energy to the person that has less (See Chapter Seven).

2. When you have "wanted" to leave but at the same time "felt" you should stay, was it you or the other person who really wanted you to stay? Does it happen over and over with the same people? Write down their names.

3. If you continue to think about people after they are out of sight, then you have a "corded" connection between you that both of you will carry until something of a higher priority in your subconscious takes its place.

You affect many people's lives every day of your life. You make a difference in just being here. You can help every person in this world with THEIR fears by facing YOUR fears.

Each bit of knowledge that every one of us learns goes into a pool of knowledge that is a sum total; anyone can draw upon it just by using their thinking processes with intention and deep desire.

**IF YOU STOP THE CONFLICT AND WAR
THAT IS GOING ON INSIDE YOU, YOU WILL STOP
THE WAR IN THE WORLD OUTSIDE YOU**

By understanding yourself and loving yourself, and then creating change by thinking of new positive actions as often as possible, you are in fact changing your world. By changing YOUR world you are changing the external world you live in. If you stop the conflict and war that is going on inside you, you stop the war in the world outside you.

Allow it to be okay when you think thoughts that are not the kind that you wish to think. The moment you are aware of thinking those thoughts, change your thinking again with deep intent and desire. IT WILL CHANGE YOUR LIFE AND THE LIVES OF THOSE YOU LOVE. Every thought you think is a decision made by you, consciously or unconsciously, to participate in this world. No matter what you choose, your thoughts indicate how you are participating in this world.

MONITORING YOURSELF IS ONE OF THE MOST VALUABLE INVESTMENTS YOU WILL EVER MAKE

If you will monitor every second of your thinking and actions for a year-and-a-half, it will be one of the best investments you have ever made. In order to do this you must keep a watch on your thoughts, feelings and emotions on a second-by-second basis. Store the information you want to keep; cancel the information that is no longer useful. To cancel information when a thought, emotion, or idea comes into your mind that is negative, just use a word that to you is powerful enough to erase what you have just said, thought, or felt. "Cancel" is the word I use.

Once you have the word that you are going to use to cancel negative thoughts, then every time a negative thought occurs, or you say a negative statement, or make a negative judgment, say the word, "stop" or "cancel" or "no" . . . whatever the word is that you have chosen. If you are in a place where you cannot speak the word out loud, then say it with your mind with strong desire and intent.

"Monitoring" means watching what you think, hear, and accept, as well as what you say and what you believe. Watch carefully what you say and listen to what you say, not in fear of what others may think, but with the knowledge that you can change your life by redirecting your thoughts on a second-by-second basis.

YOU ARE WORTH INVESTING IN

If you say you do not have time for this, I will honor your right to feel or say that, but consider the fact that you are worth investing in. **By investing time and energy in yourself for your present life, you are creating your future as well.** You CAN make the time to change your life. There is not one person on this planet that can do it as well as you can.

As an ultra-sensitive you have denied your emotions many times. You have held back your needs, wants, hopes and desires. You have been overwhelmed by your emotions. You have lived the emotions of others. It seemed at times that, if your emotions would just stop or go away, life would be so much easier.

Your emotions are a natural part of you. They are a gift that will help you understand and relate to others. When they are balanced and brought into control by you, your emotions are the door to all the things you want to be.

First, own your emotions as a positive tool. Know that it is acceptable (and many times preferable) to be emotionally expressive. You as an ultra-sensitive have been told by life in many different ways that you are too sensitive for your own good. The message is that you are too sensitive to live a healthy, happy, successful life as a capable adult. That message is not true. I am finding out more each day, as many other ultra-sensitives are also finding out, that ultra-sensitivity is a key and tool to real strength. Not "over-emotions" but "ultra-sensitivity."

I have found many other ultra-sensitives who feel even MORE deeply because they have gained control and mastery of themselves. They have accepted their ultra-sensitivity and opened up to a happy, free, and loving world. They have given up trying to control others and have concentrated on controlling themselves, their lives and their emotions without suppresssing or limiting themselves in any area.

EXERCISES

Choose One Exercise or the Other Depending on Your Obstacles to Positive Ultra-sensitivity:

1. **If you are emotional,** watch a movie and stop yourself from becoming emotional. Concentrate on not getting caught up in the movie.

2. **If you cannot be emotional in a movie,** keep working with yourself until you can feel the emotions of the characters in the movie.

3. **If you are logically minded,** move yourself out of your logic and get lost in the story emotionally without watching the movie analytically.

Watch yourself to see when you become involved or uninvolved in the movie. When do your emotions connect or disconnect? Can you connect or disconnect? Do you have to watch the entire movie no matter how good or bad it is? Can you start and stop your emotions when you are watching a movie when you want to? Or is it possible only when the tension or emotions of the movie have changed to another scene? Practicing in this way can help you to observe yourself and help you to disconnect.

11 How to Handle Money Spiritually

MONEY IS SIMPLY ENERGY. It is a tool we use to buy things from people when we do not have what they need in exchange. So we use the tool called money instead of an article to trade. Money is a way for us to have our value acknowledged in the physical world. Money is also a way for us to be shown that we have no value at all. When people are willing to give us their emotional support but not their money, the message they are giving us is that they are willing to acknowledge us in the emotional world but not the physical world. When we are unwilling to deal with money, we are telling everyone—including ourselves—that we do not want to be in this physical world.

As ultra-sensitives we are not willing to see value in the physical world because it has denied us for so long. In turn, we do not receive value for the things we do.

MONEY IS A WAY FOR US TO HAVE OUR VALUE ACKNOWLEDGED IN THE PHYSICAL WORLD

Then we end up being hurt because we gave with a loving thought and it was not given back to us in equal value. We did not expect anything material back; what we really wanted was not the money but the acknowledgement. When ultra-sensitives do not receive either, they become hurt or angry or both.

MONEY IS ALSO A WAY FOR US TO BE SHOWN THAT WE HAVE NO VALUE AT ALL

Money can be a spiritual tool if it is used in a constructive way to enhance your life rather than limit it. To live in this physical world you need money to survive. There are opportunities to trade, but even in trade you will find the same obstacles to face, overcome and conquer. Trade is another way to receive value for value—or to receive something of less value.

Many times spiritual people say, "I can live without money," or "I don't need money," or "Money isn't important to me." I agree that money should not be the driving force for your life. But to be a true spiritual being you need the ability to use **all** the tools in the universe. Not using money is like a warrior of ancient times saying he would fight with only his own weapon and no other; or a teacher saying s/he will teach only three truths and no others. The more you avoid using money, the more it will come back to you to face until you can handle it with no attachment either way. Money is just one tool of many to use in this universe.

There can be an attachment to money simply by having pride in the fact that you can live without it. Some people feel the need to show the world how strong they are, and enduring poverty is a sign of their achievement in their unspoken goal toward proving their humility. That is an attachment. Some people feel a sense of pride in the fact that they are more spiritual because they do not have money; they feel that this denial makes them more spiritual. Those belief systems come not only from past beliefs from ancient cultures in connection with religion, but from some present-day spiritual beliefs as well.

The attachment to poverty works AGAINST a person's spiritual development; working spiritually with money must be faced sooner or later. It is against your spiritual development to have an attachment to material things which include money. "Attachment" means that you feel that you cannot live without your material possessions; it does not mean that you feel you should not have them.

Money is not evil. Money is not the root of all evil. What people do with money can be evil. What people do to create money to prove their value in the material world can be evil. What people believe of money can be evil. But money of itself is not evil. Money is simply a tool to be used wisely for good. Money can also be used in unwise ways against the good of one or more persons. It is what people do with money that makes it good or bad. The tool itself is neither good nor bad.

Money is a measurement of value in the physical world. The problem begins when one person is not willing to give equal value to another person for services rendered or goods exchanged. It is important for you to treat a penny as wisely as you would treat a hundred or thousand dollar bill.

The way you work with money, use money and share it with others is the way you will receive it back. ONLY IF YOU VALUE YOURSELF EQUALLY IN YOUR DEALINGS WITH MONEY WILL YOU RECEIVE BACK WHAT YOU GIVE SO FREELY. If you are unwilling to give to yourself, if you do not take time for yourself, if you save the least for yourself and give the best to others, then that is the way money will come back to you.

GIVE UP ALWAYS LEAVING YOURSELF FOR LAST

Money will come to you only if you are willing to give it to yourself by taking time to do things you like to do. Buy things you truly like instead of "making do" or saying that something is good enough when in truth you really do not like it at all. Give up the "martyr energy" of always leaving yourself for last. These are all value measurements that say spiritually TO yourself FROM yourself that you do not count.

If you do not mean much to yourself, then money will not return back to you no matter how many times you give it out to others. Even if others want to give to you, in some way you will block it if it creates more value in you than you are willing to give to yourself.

The message you are giving yourself is that you are not worth much—that you do not really matter. The

HOW YOU TREAT YOURSELF IS HOW YOU TELL
OTHERS TO TREAT YOU

message I would like you to give to yourself is that YOU
REALLY DO COUNT. That you are worth a great deal
and equal to all people. That you deserve to receive the
abundance of the universe. Not just in money but in all
things. Once you receive this knowlege and information for yourself, then your children and your loved
ones have a better chance to understand and accept it for
themselves. We always want the best things for those we
love, but WE are their example in all areas of our
life . . . and that includes our attitude toward giving
and receiving money. What we say is important, but
WHAT WE ARE and HOW WE LIVE OUR LIVES gives the
strongest message of all.

How many times have you found yourself following the same money patterns your parents did, even
when you said you would never do that. Those money
patterns were instilled in you by your parents' actions
even more strongly than their words. When you change
the patterns that are creating obstacles in your life, you
are giving your loved ones more of a chance to create
positive patterns in their lives. Every change you make
gives everyone in this world the opportunity for that
same change. It is the right of every individual to choose
to make a change or not, but because of YOUR changes
you have opened the door for others. Even though this
is true, remember to make your changes for yourself and
no one else.

Everyone wants to be a good person. Ultra-
sensitives, even more than others, want to be good

because they feel, know or see the pain of others. We are taught in many ways that the good will inherit the earth, but somehow what seems to go along with that is the idea that you have to be poor to be good, which is not true. I have met many good people from all walks of life and from all different cultures. They have been wealthy as well as living without any home or material possessions. They all were good, loving, human beings who cared about people and the world they lived in. The people that had chosen the simplicity of life had earlier created wealth in this lifetime. They chose a path where their life was taken care of financially while they made their choice to live simply. It was taken care of by them and by what they created.

Many wealthy people have created their own wealth or respected what they had been given and continued to honor it by taking care of it as a trust. They live their lives with love and respect for people in the world and do all they can to help without causing more problems by their helping. They make those they help strong by giving help that will strengthen them and not create dependency. They help people go into business for themselves by creating a loan that the people can pay back as their business improves. They help people gain an education or go to training schools. If people who are wealthy are not doing that, it simply means that they are still in the learning process.

Personal Attitudes That Will NOT Help People Move Their Money Obstacles

1.   I will do it for them.

2.   I am afraid for them, and let them know it, if not by my words then by my actions or what I do not say.
3.   I let them know their weaknesses by reminding them how they have failed in the past.
4.   I make them feel they cannot do it without me. I say things like, "Let me do that and call me when you're ready for the next thing."
5.   I see that what they are facing is too hard for them. I tell them that by my anxiety, the fear on my face, and by calling them two and three times a day.
6.   I tell them how I overcame the same problem, but I do not listen to them or hear how they want or need to solve their problem.
7.   I am unwilling to walk them through their pain when they are ready to change and move forward.

Personal Attitudes That WILL Help People Move Their Money Obstacles

1.   Help them to SEE their next step, NOT DO IT for them.
2.   Tell them your concern and reassure them they can do it. (Remember—they really CAN or they would not have chosen that obstacle.)
3.   Support them in their strength by reminding them of their past strengths and achievements.
4.   Say to them, "I know you can do this and I will help you in any way that I can. Call me when you need me."

5.   Say to them, "Look at all your past obstacles and
     how strong they have made you. This also will
     strengthen you."
6.   Listen to them and the way they intend to face their
     problems. Let them work it out verbally while you
     listen. Give help or advice only when they ask for
     it.
7.   Be willing to walk with them through their pain if
     they are willing to change. If they are unwilling to
     change, love them in their right to make the choice
     not to change.

**What are some of the many ways that you can love
yourself?** By treating yourself well in your daily life, and
allowing others to treat you well also. You give yourself
messages when you settle for something that you really
do not want; even though it may be close to what you do
want, it does not bring a sense of joy into your heart.
Buy the very thing you want as often as possible or do
not buy anything at all.

By making yourself equal with others, you will
teach the ones you love the most. You can still be an
open, loving, and giving person. But give as much time
to yourself as you give to your family. Take time for
your own spiritual development or personal development, which are one and the same.

Say "no" to things that you really do not want to
do. Do not agree with anyone that is being negative
about you in any way, except that they have the right to
believe the way they choose to believe. Recognize your
achievements and reward yourself by an acknowledgement in the moment. Make yourself look the very best

you can, and you will show that you do value yourself
in the world. Loving yourself is a value measurement
that brings prosperity into your life.

Weekly Check-up To See How I Valued Myself

1.   How much time have I allowed for myself this
     week? Hours? Minutes?
2.   How many things did I do that I wanted to do?
     (Make a list).
3.   Were there times that I accepted second best?
     What were they? Restaurant? Grocery store? School?
     Other?
4.   How many times did I say "yes" when I wanted to
     say "no?" What were those times? How could I
     have said, "no?" Who was involved and where was
     it?

Be very conscious in your use of money. When you
have made an arrangement or commitment to another
person, be very clear on the details. Go over them step by
step. Ask the person what s/he meant. Clarify every
point so there is no confusion later. Most ultra-
sensitives do not want to bother with details because
they are conceptual beings. Because every friendship
means a great deal to you, pay attention to the details if
you want to retain the friendship or partnership.
Everyone's understanding of what should happen is
different.

Ten years ago I traded some of my work for one day
of painting. I talked with the person about what needed

to be done. I bought the paint and was ready for the trade. The only details we discussed were that he would do some painting for the work that I had done for him. He showed up two hours late to start work. He worked for twenty minutes and then went to lunch. When he finished painting the deck he had left spots on it that were unpainted, and he left the paint brushes in the sun.

At first I was angry and felt that he had not valued what I had traded with him at all. It was not until several years later that I received the "Ah ha" from that experience. I had not valued him OR myself by not making clear exactly what the trade was. I did not ask him what his hourly rate for painting was, nor did I ask his experience. I did not make clear before I did the work for him what the value of my work was to me. We did not clarify what the equal trade was for both of us. I did not state what I wanted the finished deck to look like.

I also did not state that clean-up was part of our trade. He ended up feeling that he had worked too hard for what he received, and I ended up feeling that I valued him more then he valued me . . . until I got my "Ah ha" several years later. I realized that I did not value myself OR him because I did not create the right set of circumstances for a positive trade. At the time I tried to feel that it had all happened for the best, but that was not the way I felt inside. Now I know he did not take advantage of me. I showed lack of value of him and myself by not being clear with both of us in the beginning.

How To Trade So It Really Works

Set an equal trade for both people, even if one makes more per hour than the other. Here is a list of things that will help you to work out the details of an equal trade.

1. Your hourly rate is $5.00 per hour.
2. My hourly rate is $10.00 per hour.
3. I will work 1 hour for 2 hours of your work.
4. You will work 2 hours, from noon to 2:00 p.m., on Monday, September 10, 1993.
5. Cleaning up your tools (or other specific things) will be part of the trade.
6. The work you do will be totally finished in a way we both agree to ahead of time.
7. I will trade 1 hour of my work when you have completed your end of the trade. My time will be Tuesday, September 11, 1993. I will work from 10:00 a.m. to 11:00 a.m.

If your money is not working for you and yet you are putting everything you know into it, the answer is that you are not seeing the physical world information. In one of the areas that I work, one of the many special people I work with was having difficulty with money. She did everything she knew to make her new profession a success. She loved her work. She believed in herself. She created beautiful brochures. She talked to people about her work. She saw the value of her work. She set up an office that was perfect for her work. She got positive feedback on the work that she had done, but it all was not coming together fast enough for her to pay her bills.

Because it was not working, she was wondering what she was doing wrong. She was quick to understand that she had not left room for the PHYSICAL WORLD TIMING to cause her business to work in the material world. She was in a "people business" that worked through word of mouth as well as brochures, and it was simply a matter of time before her business would work. If she would only give it the time that was needed on the physical world plane, it would be a success. She did everything that she knew to do; now she had to support it in the material world until it could stand on its own just like any business.

Using spiritual principles still means that it must be God's time, no matter what we do or think. It must also filter down to the physical world and fit into the physical world laws of timing, cause and effect. God's time is her God Within's time to manifest the abundance that is hers. She had to do everything she could on the physical realm to make that happen, which even meant getting a part-time job to support her belief in herself until her business could stand by its own power.

GET RID OF OUTMODED BELIEF SYSTEMS
ABOUT MONEY

It is important to clean closets in order to make room for the new abundance that is coming into your life. Yes, physical house closets, but also mental closets. These are belief systems that are getting in the way of the abundance that you are deserving to receive:

judgments of other people and how they use their money; beliefs on how you use your money or should use your money; judgments and beliefs on what money is.

Get rid of outmoded belief systems that include the belief that money tarnishes everythings it touches; the belief that you are not supposed to have money this lifetime; the belief that you never got your chance and never will; the belief that everything is against your success. Release yourself from the fear of having money.

If you are not sure whether you have this fear or not, then check out what you do when you have extra money. If you spend it as fast as you accumulate it (even if you don't FEEL the fear of it), it is still fear. Fear hides behind the smoke screens of depression, boredom and emotional pain. The best way to move through fear is with action, even if the action is in very small steps.

Movement is movement no matter how slow, like the movement in a pane of glass. When I saw a pane of antique glass, I wanted to know what the waves were in the glass. I was told that glass moves, and that the movement is so slow that it shows only in very old glass. The older it gets the wavier it becomes. But that movement is still movement. Like the antique glass it does not matter how slowly you move, it matters only THAT you move.

In ancient times priests had to take a vow of poverty to show they were free of the material world. In my work I have found that most spiritual people have taken a vow of poverty that is still operating in this day and age. Even though you may not be in a poverty state, you may still have just enough to survive, no matter what your lifestyle.

The priests of old were taught to ask for their bowl of rice each day in order to prove their faith and trust in God. In our soul memory we still believe that we should have just enough and no more.

Even though we are not priests in this day and age, the vow we took in past lives centuries ago is still operating in our lives right along with the present-day life beliefs that we were taught in childhood. Our patterns were not always taught in words. Most of the time they were taught by the example of how the authority figures in our lives viewed and handled money.

RELEASE YOUR VOW OF POVERTY FROM ANCIENT TIME OR PRESENT TIME

In order to release yourself from your vow of poverty, use the power of the word. Say your words out loud.

1. Ask and you will receive.
2. Renounce your vow of poverty by declaration.
3. Renounce your vow verbally, physically with desire. Use this affirmation:

I now renounce my vow of poverty and still claim my God-given right to spiritual development. I now take a vow of abundance to show forth for all people my Divine right to have and share God's abundance as my own.

Be as willing to receive as you are to give. Many people with money lessons to learn are very loving and willing to give, but they are not as willing (or not willing at all) to receive. It is your gift to others that you trust them enough to receive a gift from them. It is important that you neither feel nor put strings on the gift that is given to you no matter in what way the gift was given to you. To judge a gift is still a judgment that will come back to you. The karma will still be yours even if the gift was given with strings. If you do not judge the strings, then you will not have to deal with the karma of those strings. If the other person, in truth, has put strings on the gift, s/he will have to balance the karma of those strings. It is also true that you always have the right to refuse a gift and wait for another day for that "opportunity-to-learn" to come back to you, wearing the same face, but perhaps on a totally different person.

If you accept a gift in all love and sincerity, then no one and nothing can take the loving acceptance of that gift away from you except yourself. No one can make a fool out of you or trick you unless you let them by letting your judgment rule you instead of living your life with an accepting heart. If you have accepted something in sincerity, then nothing can change the fact that you accepted the gift with a loving and open heart, willing to trust the moment.

It is usually only other people's opinions that cause you to change your mind about the event or gift that was given. Before you shared with others you were totally delighted with the gift. Sometimes after sharing with others the gift seems to have become tarnished somehow. The only thing that has changed were the other person's words that were spoken and the way you have accepted those words. This is another example of the power of words to change your life. **Since words can change your perspective, they can also change your life.**

12 Living With Your Body: Sensitivity, Spirituality and Food

Listen to Your Body

THE FIRST WARNING system of your body is your nose. Your sense of smell is there to help you to recognize what is good for you to eat. No matter how good the food looks and no matter how good the food tasted last time you ate it, no matter who fixed it for you, no matter how much they love you, no matter how wonderfully they cook, if your nose tells you that the food does not smell good, then do not eat it.

The fact that the food does not smell good to you does not mean that there is anything wrong with the food for anyone else, but it does mean that that food is not good for your body and is not compatible with your body. It may make you sick. Honor your body and recognize that it is doing its job very well. If you make a decision to override the information from the body, then that is your right and your choice.

LISTENING TO MY BODY TELLS ME HOW WELL IT CAN WORK WITH ME

I have learned through my experiences in the past eighteen years that my body knows exactly what it is doing. Even when I make a choice that is not good for my body, it does not work against me. In the past I have made many choices that were harmful to my body. Even in the present I will choose against what I know my body wants. More and more I am willing to listen to my body and change my patterns of eating, resting and playing for the good of my whole being.

During the last two-and-a-half years I have lost 130 pounds by listening to my body. I have not starved my body or abused it to achieve this weight loss. I have talked to my body. I have listened to my body. I have appreciated my body more than I have at any other time in my life. My body is a wonderful tool and vessel that carries my spirit.

The next system to listen to is your sense of taste. Your tongue is designed to help you taste food. If any food or drink that you place on your tongue does not taste good, then do not eat it, even though everyone else that eats it says it tastes great. I used to say, "There isn't a food that I don't like."

What I found out to be true was that I did not feel I had the right to dislike any food because that was the way I was raised as a child. Now I know that there are many foods and kinds of foods that I truly do not like and that it is perfectly okay. If the food did not taste right to me, I always used to assume that something was wrong with my taste rather than that something was wrong with the food.

I used to be afraid I would hurt people's feeling by not eating their food. I was also raised to believe that if I did not eat everything on my plate, the children in other countries would starve. I was made to feel that I should be grateful that I had food to eat because the starving children did not have anything to eat. This taught me that I had no right of choice and I should be grateful for what I had. I have since changed those emotional belief systems, so now I know that when I do not choose, then I am allowing circumstances, events, or people in my life to make my choices for me.

EATING EVERYTHING ON MY PLATE WILL NOT HELP THE STARVING CHILDREN OF THE WORLD

To replace the pattern of feeling that you must eat everything on your plate, do this: Every time you eat, leave a little food on your plate to show that you know there is abundance for you and also for everyone in the world. **Your overeating will not bring food to starving people.** Then, with the abundance that comes to you from your new thinking/creating/acting pattern, you can actively get involved or send money that will create food for all people everywhere.

You can also spend at least ten minutes a day in thought about how people can be fed all over the world in positive ways that will help everyone. Because you are CREATING your world with your thinking, you can also CHANGE your world with your thinking. Once you change your world, the result is that the external world you live in will also change. Yes. You must live realistically in the present. But you do not have to believe or think or feed the negative events or things that are happening.

TAKING CHARGE OF MY THOUGHTS TEN MINUTES A DAY CAN CHANGE SUFFERING IN THE WORLD

By changing your belief system at this time, you will change the idea that what is happening today will continue to happen tomorrow. It is not by accident that the most powerful books in the world either start with—or mention somewhere within them the power of the word. For example: **In the beginning was the Word, and the Word was with God, and the Word was God (John 1:1).** Changing the words you use and the thoughts you think is the way to change the world. Combine this with changing your actions to respect yourself more and to show more respect for all living beings.

Listen to your body when it has sufficient food. Whether you are thin or overweight or the perfect weight for you, listen to your body. Hear when it is full. If you eat for emotional reasons, then let yourself taste every bite with pleasure. Do not reprimand yourself with each bite. When you are eating emotionally, if you do not allow yourself the emotional pleasure of the first bite of food, or the second bite, or the pleasure of any of the food, you will not ever get full. You are not eating for emptiness of the physical body; you are eating because of your emptiness of emotions.

OVERFILLING WITH FOOD IS A SEDATIVE TO QUIET OUR FEELINGS

Another reason that overweight ultra-sensitives overeat is to desensitize themselves so they will not feel so deeply about things that are bothering them. There are many people that are their perfect size that still eat the way an overweight person does. They criticize themselves for every bite of food they eat, and do not give themselves the emotional pleasure of eating a certain food. If you allow yourself the full pleasure of eating what you want to eat, then you will not overeat nor will you need to eat that food every day.

Many ultra-sensitives who are too thin do not like to eat food because it causes them to come back into their bodies and be grounded. They do not like the full feeling it gives them because it makes them feel as if they are going to be too slow, and then they will not have all the information they need to protect themselves from danger. This is usually a learned habit from childhood when they were punished and they did not really understand why. They feel that if they do not eat they will stay totally aware and will be prepared to learn what they need to know in order not to be punished. It is very much like athletes who keep themselves on the edge of what they consider their "peak performance" mode, ready to compete at any moment.

I believe from my own experiences—as well as many other people's experiences—that we eat certain foods because of the result we get in our bodies. We do not always eat food to be thin or overweight. I have found from my own past experiences that when I wanted chocolate it was just after I had had an emotional experience that was draining, or during a time when I was feeling especially good about myself. During that time I had a fear of my power and of feeling powerful.

The chocolate grounds my energy while the sugar in the chocolate expands me so I can feel free. The butter in chocolate slows down my ultra-sensitivity so that I can have some space from feeling every emotion or feeling that comes along. There is also a euphoria that comes from eating chocolate that is in the chocolate itself. So when I wanted that exact result I would eat chocolate.

I also learned my eating patterns from my family. They taught me what so called "goodies" were, and when I deserved a reward. I always received chocolate at Easter, Christmas, and Valentine's Day as a gift. This taught me that chocolate was something special. So when I ate chocolate then I was also special. I was also taught that I was bad if I ate too much, so when I needed to feel badly about myself I also ate too much food or too much chocolate. Then I usually ate enough so that I knew that I had eaten too much so I could really feel badly about myself.

YOU EAT FOOD OR DO NOT EAT FOOD FOR THE
SPECIFIC EFFECT IT CREATES

I have since changed my patterns in connection with chocolate and now it no longer has the deep emotional appeal that it used to have for me. I have taken the emotional reasons for eating chocolate and changed them. I have transferred those beliefs to balanced, good food.

I eat salads when I want my thinking to be clear and when I do not want to be bogged down or feel heavy. I used to eat beef when I wanted to drown my emotions. I also used other proteins when I wanted to slow down my ultra-sensitivity. I used to eat or drink sugar when I needed to feel free—when too many things were coming at me too fast and I started feeling as though everything were out of control and demanding things of me I could not do. I now eat fruit when I want energy and vitality. Fruits also clean my system of toxins.

I eat vegetables for the energy and endurance that help my system, without causing a drain on my emotional or spiritual energy. I eat grains when I need to feel in touch with the earth cycles and the earth itself. I now eat fish when I feel the need for grounding. It helps back up the new training in my mind that now takes over. I had used food totally before with very little mind training.

Your body is the perfect mirror for what is going on inside of your mind. Whatever physical problem you are having in your body or on your body is your spirit's

YOUR BODY IS THE PERFECT MIRROR FOR WHAT
IS HAPPENING TO YOU EMOTIONALLY,
MENTALLY, OR SPIRITUALLY

way of telling you that something is wrong in another part of your being. If it is your eye, then there is something that you are emotionally not seeing. If it is your left eye, then it is about something that you left behind or something in your past. If it is underneath your eye, then it is telling you there is something right under your eye or eyes that you are not seeing. If it is your right eye then it may have something to do with something that you do not feel right about seeing; or it is something that is happening in your life right now.

Nearsighted people need their rewards immediately and cannot wait for long-range goals like farsighted people can. Nearsighted people are excellent at seeing short-range or immediate goals. I am nearsighted. Since I have gained this understanding, I now have less difficulty than I used to with goal-setting, and I am better able to create long-range goals. I intend to continue working on that. It is easier for me to think "in the moment" than in the future for my own life, even though I read future guidelines for others. Usually, farsighted people have difficulty in thinking about their own life goals in the moment, but are excellent in looking at long-range goals.

If the right side of your body is having a problem, that can mean that there is something in your life that you do not feel right about. It can also mean that something or someone is taking your rights away. If it is the left side of your body, it can mean that something from the past is still affecting you and you need to see what that is in order to heal that part of yourself. If it is your left side it can also mean that you feel you are being left out or you feel left out. The left side of your body is your masculine side and the right side of your body is feminine. The importance of the masculine-feminine information is that it tells you how your internal masculine or internal feminine systems are existing within you. It lets you know whether they are in health and happiness or if not, what degree of pain they are in. It also shows you where the problem with your health exists in connection with what is going on in your life.

YOUR BODY TALKS TO YOU WITH PAIN IN ORDER TO BE HEARD

If there is a problem with your legs, it has something to do with movement. If there is a problem with your back, it has something to do with a burden you are carrying. If there is a problem with your arms, it has to do with movement that is within your reach, but that you are not doing it or reaching for it.

If there is a problem with your ears, it can mean that there is something you need to hear or that you are not hearing . . . a message that is usually about yourself from yourself. If there is a problem in your throat, it can mean there is something you need to say. Perhaps you need to speak out, speak up or speak in front of groups of people. Problems with your joints mean that you need to be more flexible in your thinking and in your life about judging yourself or others. You need to love yourself more and see the good that you do and the good that is in you.

If there is a problem in your circulatory system, it means you need to give more to yourself and be more willing to receive from others—their knowledge, information and insight—and see the value in it. If there is a problem in the lymphatic system, it means you need to clean thoughts, ideas, judgments, and perhaps the kinds of people you have in your life, out of your life.

If there is a problem in the heart area, you need to be more in touch with your emotions. Either you need to feel, experience or understand your emotions better, or you need to bring your emotions under training and under your own control.

It is not your ultra-sensitivity but your "over emotions" that are creating the feeling of being taken advantage of. Even if you are being taken advantage of, you can change that by changing yourself.

WHENEVER YOU FEEL ABSOLUTE ABOUT ANYTHING TO THE DEGREE THAT YOU FEEL IT SHOULD NEVER CHANGE . . . THERE IS USUALLY A DESTRUCTIVE EMOTIONAL SYSTEM HIDING BEHIND THAT TRUTH

If you have a liver or kidney problem, it may mean that you need to eliminate some things from your life that you felt were absolutely necessary. You might even be feeling that "this is exactly the way life has to be." Whenever you feel absolute about anything to the degree that it should never change, it is important to look at that belief system because there is usually a destructive emotional system hiding behind that limited truth. When you have a truth in your life that you are willing to look at or to discuss without fear of losing it, then it is your truth and there are no destructive emotional systems hiding within it.

If you have a problem with your knees it means you are not getting your needs met. If it is the left knee, it means you have not had your needs met in the past. If it is the right knee, it means you are not having your needs met in the present. If it is both knees then that means that you have not had your needs met in the past or in the present.

If you have a problem with your big toe it means that your emotional thinking about the past is not balanced. If you have a problem with your right big toe it means that your emotional thinking about your present is not balanced in some area of your life or in some way.

If you have problems with your left elbow it usually means that you bent in an emotional direction in the past that you feel badly about or are in pain about. If it is your right elbow, it usually means that you are bending in the present time in areas that you are not feeling good about or that you are hurting about.

If you are emotionally ultra-sensitive, remember that your body is ultra-sensitive also, but that does not mean it has to have problems. It just means that it is a finely-tuned instrument that needs more care and attention in order to run at its peak performance.

13 Sexuality and Spirituality

SEXUAL ENERGY BEGINS in the base of the spine. The only difference between sexual energy and spiritual energy is the way your mind directs it. Your chakras or energy centers are the energy network that transmute sexual to spiritual energy by starting at the lower centers and traveling to the higher centers.

There are many different explanations for the energy centers of the body. All the information is valid, but you should not try to intermix different theories in order to try to make sense out of one of them. You will be able to compare each idea with another idea but I do not recommend that you try to make them all interrelate with one another.

There is a belief that there are seven energy centers. There is also a belief that there are nine energy or "chakra" centers. There is also a belief that there are

twelve energy centers with only seven directly connected to the physical body with the rest being all spiritual
centers connected to each person. The twelve-energy-
centers-of-the-body information works better for me
and makes more sense to me than the others do, as a
more complete idea. But in speaking about sexual
energy I will just speak about the seven chakras or
energy centers connected to the body. Our sexual energy
and our spiritual energy both start from our root or base
chakra.

It is our brain/mind that converts the sexual
energy at the base or root chakra to spiritual energy by
the way our mind thinks about what we want to do. All
energy starts out as sexual energy or "life force energy"
and then is changed as our thinking is changed or
redirected into whatever is happening in our life. When
we release energy from our base chakra it becomes more
refined the higher it travels up our energy centers.

When it is in the base chakras, we are focused on
sexual energy or "life survival" directions. When we
have moved the energy from the base chakras to the
spleen chakra our motivation is changed and directed
toward endings and beginnings in our life. It is also
directed into eliminating the things, thoughts, ideas or
actions that are outmoded in our life.

**MANY TIMES WE NEED TO FIND SOMEONE TO
TALK TO SO WE CAN HEAR OUR OWN WORDS**

The next energy center or chakra is the solar plexus
center. This center is the emotional center where we feel

most of our emotional responses. This is the area we feel response in when something unexpected hits us.

The solar plexus center has been helpful to me in gathering my emotions together when I have been "corded" by another person or by my own need for a connection. If I do my breathing exercises and focus on clearing this center by using my name and the mantra to clear the chakras (Chapter Five) I can "disconnect." I have also found it helpful to place both hands, one on top of the other, on top of the solar plexus center and breathe three slow, easy, deep breaths. This helps me to center or ground myself so I can relate to the physical world. It is best to do this exercise until you feel connected and grounded. Sometimes I have to do this exercise six or seven times before I really feel connected to this earth.

The next energy center is the heart center. This is also called the heart chakra. With this energy center you can feel/know, give and receive unconditional love: love with no strings attached. When you want someone truly to hear you, and you mean what you are saying sincerely, then you want to concentrate on speaking from the heart center, on working on actually feeling your voice coming out of the heart center.

The way to do this is to concentrate on the heart center and take three deep, easy, slow breaths. Put your mind in touch with your heart center. Another way to say that is to think from your heart center when you wish to speak from there. Once you have focused your thoughts on each center and raised your energy to the heart center, then your connection with the other person will reflect loving friendship more than sexual energy, even with a lover, partner or mate.

THE THROAT ENERGY CENTER HELPS YOU TO
SPEAK AND BE HEARD

The next energy center is the throat chakra. The throat chakra is the energy center that helps you to speak and be heard. It empowers your words to help you to communicate clearly with yourself as well as others. Many times we need to find someone to say things to so we can hear the words come back to us. Many times the way other people receive our words causes us to take our words more seriously. When you have raised the sexual energy to the throat energy center effectively, then you can heal with your words.

The next energy center is the brow chakra, or as many people refer to it, the "third eye." This energy center is your "spiritual eye." It is the center to see clearly your spiritual guides, your spiritual development, your spiritual teacher and your spiritual truth. When your sexual energy reaches this level effectively you can see visions and have more solid soul-projection experiences, which some people refer to as "out of body" experiences. When this energy center is thoroughly developed, you can create the miracles that were manifested by many of the great teachers.

The last of the energy centers that I will mention in this book is the crown chakra. This chakra is considered the mysterious energy center of the body. It is considered the pure spiritual center. It is thought by some to be the center that our eternal soul is connected to our physical body with. When you can raise your sexual or life force energy to this level you can—over a period of time—create a physical body to live in that does not decay.

Sexual energy is a life force energy that is to be used to re-create the race. It is to be used to renew a commitment between two people who love one another. It is to remind us, during that beautiful time of union with someone we love, of a higher and truer union with our God-Self or Universal-Self. Sexual energy in each and every one of us can be used to heal any and all parts of our body once we learn how to direct our total energy to achieve the mind training that is necessary. So many times we are ready to listen but not ready to apply ourselves to do the repetitive work that is necessary to achieve the desired results.

The best way to regenerate sexual energy is by the use of breathing exercises. The best kinds of breathing exercises are those that are taught by teachers who teach voice control and training. It is important for you to know that in the healing of yourself or others, you must have control of your voice in order to achieve results that are lasting. "Control" means that under all and any kinds of stress you can direct your voice and have it create the exact tone that you want, when you want, and for as long as you want. The foods you eat also will block or open up your sexual energy; a healthy body will have more sexual energy then an unhealthy body. If you eat foods that create energy your sexual energy will be better. If you eat foods that stifle your energy then your sexual energy will be less.

The reason I have chosen to mention sexual energy in a book on spirituality is that sexual energy is creative

UNCONDITIONAL LOVE, WHEN BACKED UP BY SEXUAL ENERGY CONVERTED INTO SPIRITUAL ENERGY, IS THE MOST POWERFUL COMBINATION IN THE UNIVERSE

energy and can be used for more than just physical sexual release. As a spiritual person, it is important for you to use your sexual energy wisely because this can speed up your spiritual development. It is not necessary to give up your sexuality and become celibate in order to become more spiritual, although I do agree that there are times that by abstaining from sexual release you can redirect this creative energy into powerful results.

It is not by accident that sexual energy is one of the two most powerful energies in the body. Sexual energy is energy manifested physically. Spiritual energy is sexual energy converted by the mind to be available when called upon for use in any part of one's life. The other powerful energy is unconditional love which, when backed up by sexual energy converted into spiritual energy, is the most powerful combination in the universe.

Sexual energy is the combination of electric and magnetic energy in your body. Electric energy in your body is male energy. It is a direct, hot, force of energy. Magnetic energy in your body is female energy. Magnetic energy is energy that is flowing, fluid, cool energy. When these two energies are united in your body, they become the God-Energy in action made manifest in your body universe. If your magnetic and electric energies are out of balance with each other, or with any other part or organ of your body, that is when illness occurs.

A unity between male and female energy is what is needed to balance the sexual energy within each person. No one can find a true balance of sexual energy to reach the point of enlightenment until all the energy centers in the body, mind, and spirit—including sexual energy— are balanced.

This takes place by finding a person, male or female, who helps to blend the sexual energy by being your true balance at that time, even if there are conflicts between you. It does not mean that to find this balance you must always be in conflict with your partner. It does mean that you must find the missing parts of yourself and come to terms with those dormant parts by awakening them. When you are ready, you will have directed your sexuality into the tool it was meant to be by bringing yourself to the threshold of enlightenment. This will happen by being in true and perfect balance within yourself with the help of another person.

If you feel complete within yourself and do not on any level have the need for a lover, partner, companion, or mate, then you are ready within yourself to bridge the gap into Self-realization. Many spiritual teachers who are near completion will suddenly be faced with their sexuality because in truth it is the last thing they have to balance within themselves, if they have not balanced it before that point in their development.

If the sexual energy is not balanced within a person by traveling from the base chakra through the crown chakra, bringing a true and perfect balance of electric and magnetic energy throughout the person, then it is not done. If a person is using her or his sexual energy with too much *electric* energy, it will create friction and cause conflict in the body or it will create too much emphasis on the sexual. If a person has too much *magnetic* energy, then that person will have very little sexual desire and will use her or his sexual energy for everything *but* physical sexual expression. Each of these ways is an extreme that will slow down the person from living a balanced, happy, true spiritual life. Sexuality is a healthy part of the physical life that brings vitality, life, and balance into each person's life.

The physical act of sexual expression creates health when it is a harmony for both partners. It is true of the homosexual relationships as well as the hetero-sexual relationships. Both kinds of relationships will bring balance into the universe. Everything is really the way it should be.

This is the reason we are going through a sexual revolution right now and there are so many conflicts in connection with sexual energy, even in the form of dis-ease. It is telling us on a very physical life level that we are not balanced in a true and healthy balance with our sexual energy, in the way we express it through our thoughts, with our emotions, with our body or with our spirit. Everything must be brought into balance in order to be healthy. Most of us are healthy in some areas, but few human beings are healthy in all areas. No one else can judge this for you; you can only perceive this for yourself.

Unless you are already in your true balance, this balance can be brought about only with another person. It does not mean that you must marry to be healthy, and it does not mean that you must have a permanent partner. What it does mean is that you must find the complement/partner for your life in order to balance all levels of yourself, and until you do, there will be a feeling of incompleteness within you. It can be one or several people (not speaking just sexually).

You may be able to set aside your need for another person in your life for a time, but it will surface again and again until you have achieved that balance within yourself. Many times in a relationship there is the feeling that you need a new relationship. Whether you stay in your present relationship or seek out a new one is not important. Your search for balance will be a driving need within you and you will continue to look for it because it is the way this physical life is designed. If we cannot bring about the balance within ourselves, then we are driven to find that person who will bring about our true balance. That is what the chemistry and attraction toward another person is all about, whether that attraction is for a moment or for lifetimes.

If you are without a partner or mate for the moment, that does not mean that you are not growing spiritually. It means that you are going through a time in your life when you need to reflect upon yourself without the input of information from a partner. In other words, you need to know who you are and what you are, in terms of getting to know your thinking and responding processes without information on a daily basis from another person, even another person you have made an agreement with or a commitment to.

You are developing whether you have another person as a partner in your life or not. You need to see how far you have progressed. You need to be able to feel or know or visualize what you need next in your life in order to feel complete. It is not wrong to have quiet periods of your life without a relationship. It is always your choice to be in a relationship or not be in a relationship. Sometimes you will choose not to be in a relationship, by choosing to fill your life with someone that is no longer in a relationship with you, and is already in a new relationship with someone else.

That is just a way of giving yourself time. Many times it is also a way to work through some things within yourself with the help of the other pseron as a past influence instead of a present one, because you need more time on that specific issue. Sometimes you will choose a relationship with someone who is not available. You do this to create the space for yourself to control the amount of contact, in order to learn about yourself, but not to learn about the other person. I have worked with people who have needed six or seven years to work through a particular relationship after they have left it. They needed to process a certain part of the relationship over and over until in truth they knew it was gone.

To bring the balance back you must look at your emotions and your inner self to see if you are using more female or male energy in your life, then bring the one back into balance with the other.

It does not matter which one needs to be brought back into balance, but one of the energies must be balanced for a healing to occur. When one of the energies is brought back into balance, then the other one is more easily balanced.

How to Know Whether My Inner-male or Inner-female is Stronger

When My Inner-Female Self is Stronger:

1. I look for support from outside myself.
2. I think I have value only if I have a male in my life.
3. I want to be taken care of by someone.
4. I am afraid to make my own decisions alone.
5. I always think of myself as supportive of someone else.
6. I think of myself last.
7. I dress to please others rather than myself.
8. If I see my role in life as mothering others.

When My Inner-Male Self is Stronger:

1. I believe I have to do it alone.
2. I keep my physical body pain to myself.
3. I suppress my emotions about my deep feelings.
4. I cannot ask for what I want, but feel I must protect and take care of others.
5. I must drive myself to achieve, no matter the price.
6. I feel that my life is never my own; it belongs to my boss and those I love.
7. I must prove I am strong by not needing anyone in my life even though I have a family.
8. I feel that everyone depends upon me for survival.

Use these lists to create the opposite patterns in your life.

These are examples of an out-of-balance male or female drive. Either one can be brought back into balance by you. First by recognition; second, by use of intent of mind; third, by use of directed will, with desire and motivation behind the will. Remember, a female can have stronger male energy and a male can have stronger female energy because of the demands their present life has made on them. At this point I am speaking of energy and not sexuality. People's past lives also have a strong influence on how their energy manifests in this life.

14 How to Live With A Sensitive or Relate to a Sensitive

LIVING WITH AN ULTRA-SENSITIVE can be a most rewarding or a most frustrating experience. To make it a rewarding experience, all you need to do is understand what motivates an ultra-sensitive toward life. There are many different kinds of ultra-sensitivity. It is important that you understand what kind of ultra-sensitive is in your life.

If you are living with or wanting to relate to a *visual ultra-sensitive*, make sure that you create visual pictures in your conversation with him or her, especially when you want to get your point across. Visual pictures are words that relay a whole picture without too much detail at first. The words you use are very important because the ultra-sensitive is not only hearing your words but is also feeling the content of your words. The ultra-sensitive is also feeling YOUR reaction to your words as well as her/his OWN reaction to your words.

If you want to speak/share/communicate with a *feeling ultra-sensitive,* it is important that you do not have feelings that you are carrying around that are about something else that you have not explained to the *feeling ultra-sensitive. Feeling ultra-sensitives* will put your emotions together with the words you are speaking when sometimes they do not belong together. That is the way *feeling ultra-sensitives* relate to the world.

ULTRA-SENSITIVES ARE NOT SLOW; THEY ARE PROCESSING MORE DETAILED INFORMATION.

They feel their feelings, interpret your feelings and their feelings, correlate all the feeling information together, and then respond to what you are saying. Ultra-sensitives are not slow; they just have more information to integrate into their *communication center* than other people do.

THE SENSITIVE IN YOUR LIFE WANTS TO BE UNDERSTOOD FIRST, ABOVE ALL OTHER THINGS

If you are wanting to explain something to ultra-sensitives but you have something else on your mind that is bothering you, they will pick up what is bothering you and feel that it is something that they did to upset you. They may feel that your being upset has something to do with them. You must explain your feelings, your anger, your frustrations and let ultra-sensitives know whether they are the source of those feelings or not. The ultra-sensitive in your life wants to be UNDERSTOOD first, above all other things.

If you are relating to *knowing ultra-sensitives* it is important to understand that even though they *know* information, they very seldom know the source for the information that they receive. It just comes to them and most of the time it proves to be true. A *knowing ultra-sensitive* does not have the sensory input of the *visual* or *feeling ultra-sensitive*. The *knowing ultra-sensitive* has to take the information on faith that it is true.

You can help this type of ultra-sensitive by helping to record the accuracy of the information received. It is important that you do this with kindness so you do not suppress *knowing ultra-sensitives*. If you do suppress them they will be afraid to risk telling you what they are experiencing. It does not mean that they always have to be right. What is important is that they need positive input to help them understand their *communication center*. If they are wrong, they need to know that it was their interpretation and not the information itself that was wrong. In other words, the basic information they received was not wrong, but rather what they connected the information to was wrong.

It will take a great deal of patience for to you learn how an ultra-sensitive reacts to life. Once you understand what drives or motivates sensitives to do the seemingly unrelated things they do, both of you will be a lot happier. There is no such thing as an unrelated event in an ultra-sensitive's life. Everything is connected to the ultra-sensitive or it is not in her/his life. Most ultra-sensitives are either very intense or completely disconnected. They can be very upset about an event in their life, but once they have resolved it within themselves, it is as though it never was a problem for them. They will forget the incident unless they feel that it may be useful in the future. Their *communication center* stores it as useful information for the future. Ultra-sensitives have a very definite order of priority that usually has little to do with the structural or expected order of the world.

I often think of my friend Dee, who lived in Walnut Creek. I called her from Napa Valley to ask if she would drive me to Oakland to pick up a book I had ordered. She asked if my car was broken. When she found out my car was fine she wanted to know if I was feeling all right. I explained that I was feeling fine. She said she would be happy to drive me. I drove from Napa Valley to Walnut Creek. Then Dee drove me to Oakland.

For weeks after that, she laughed with her friends about what I had asked her to do. If I had felt safe in driving to Walnut Creek, it seemed to her that there was not that much difference driving to Oakland, a mere twenty miles away. It did not make sense to her. To me—with my information and understanding about my ultra-sensitivity—it made perfect sense. I knew intuitively that I was safe driving a car from Napa Valley to Walnut Creek. I also knew that I was not safe driving my car that day to Oakland. I wanted to pick up my book, but saw the potential for an automobile accident that day if I had driven. I also saw that I would be safe with her driving me to Oakland.

I had many friends around me that would have been willing to drive, but I knew that with her there would be no accident for her, as well as no accident for me. Most people would not understand why I wanted her to drive me to Oakland, but ultra-sensitives consistently receive information that makes them seem to act in a peculiar or unusual way that makes no sense to anyone around them. Most of the time it does not even make sense to them.

If you, as an ultra-sensitive, are resistant to a particular thing that has not bothered you before but you just do not feel right about it now, it is important to listen to your senses. One way that you can help yourself is to keep asking questions. If you are working with other ultra-sensitives to help them understand an experience, before you start questioning them explain that you respect their feelings and you want to help them to understand the information they are receiving. Let them know also that you want to understand them. Piece their answers to your questions together until you both have a fairly clear picture of where their resistance is. The potential danger or obstacle is wherever their resistance is.

Maybe you are feeling uneasy at seeing a certain friend on a specific day. It could be that it is not dangerous to see your friend but the danger lies in the kind of transportation you choose to use to reach your friend. The danger may not be in going out to dinner, but in what was sprayed in the kitchen of the restaurant that contaminated the food. You may be the only one that the spray would make extremely ill.

As someone wanting to communicate with ultra-sensitives, please know that when you become frustrated with trying to get a point across, it usually is because you want them to see it from your perspective.

In other words, you want them to arrive at the information in the same way that you arrived at the information. If ultra-sensitives understood themselves better they would be able do that. But at this point in time ultra-sensitives usually become as frustrated with themselves as others do with them, when they do not get the information in the same way. They need to understand that they receive the same information but in a completely different way.

It is not by accident that a *structural* (that may be you) and a *conceptual* person (an ultra-sensitive) have created a relationship together. If you will both just have the patience to work together, there is so much each of you can learn from the other. Many times ultra-sensitives want you to arrive at the information with their methods and patterns of thinking. So with both of you needing each other to do it your own way, it becomes a stalemate in which neither one of you really gets what you want or need.

If you will give it time and create detailed communication between you, both of you will find a solution that satisfies what you want to accomplish. You begin differently, your process is different, but most of the time you both end up with the same conclusion. It is true that neither one of you wants to give up your perceptions of what you believe. I know from my own experience as a *conceptual ultra-sensitive* that you do not give up anything, but rather you gain both knowledge and information by thoroughly understanding the other person's methods of reaching a conclusion.

When you are giving directions to ultra-sensitives, it is important to give them only the information they need. Do not give added information or interesting information until they have the basic directions clear. Most importantly, explain if you are angry about something or someone other than them—or even if it IS them—so they can place what they are receiving about what you are feeling. They are working to learn from you. If you do not explain, they will have a tendency to get caught up in their own emotional intrepretation of the side issues.

When you tell an ultra-sensitive how to get to a location, write the directions down. This helps because although as long as they are with you the directions will make sense to them, once they leave you they will get confused. This is because they no longer have your degree of knowing and they are left with their partial understanding of the directions. In a kind, loving, and firm way, have ultra-sensitives repeat the information that you have given to them.

When they are with you they are "reading" your understanding of the directions. Once they are away from you they have only half the information they received by not getting the full directions clear within themselves. They need the full and precise directions that anyone would need who is looking for a location the first time.

If they do not have the directions written down when they get to the area they are looking for, they will panic and be filled with the fear that they have forgotten. Many times the fear and over-emotions will cause them to block the information that they DO have and cause them to turn the wrong way and get lost. Many times ultra-sensitives will have the tendency to think they have gone too far and turn around before they reach the true turnoff that they really needed.

Ultra-sensitives are not stupid. Most linear people assume that ultra-sensitives are slow in their thinking processes because they do not respond in the same way the structural person does. The ultra-sensitive is just being overloaded with incoming information and has to assimilate all sensory information and relate it to the physical world before s/he can respond or reply. If an ultra-sensitive responds before all information is correlated, then the response does not make sense to the person asking for the information, and many times does not even make sense to the ultra-sensitive.

IT IS IMPORTANT FOR ULTRA-SENSITIVES TO ACCEPT THAT THEY ARE DIFFERENT

Ultra-sensitives can learn how to deal with and understand the information coming in in a very rational and capable way, once they understand how their ultra-sensitivity systems work. It is important for ultra-sensitives to accept that they are different. They need to understand that the way they arrive at solutions may be different, but it can be just as effective.

When looking for information, ultra-sensitives *open up* their intuitive channels. When they *open up*, information floods in from the area they are in, and from the people they are around, whether they know the people or not. In that open state they also receive information from all the people they love and from whatever their loved ones are doing, especially if their loved ones are in any kind of confusion, problems or pain.

When ultra-sensitives reach out to someone or something that they want to learn something from, they open themselves up to every connection and cord that they have ever established in their existence. The information that comes in is sifted in order of "survival priority" or "love priority" to what is most important to the ultra-sensitive at that exact moment. These priorities can be in a constant state of change or flux according to their needs, wants, or desires.

One of my experiences happened with my son Allen when he was seven years old. It occured during a time when I did not understand my ultra-sensitivity or my children's ultra-sensitivity. I was in a city thirty-five miles away from my home, visiting some friends. My son was staying with my aunt and uncle. My aunt and uncle went to visit some friends and took him with them. It was a new area and he had not been there before so he did not know the area.

My aunt cautioned my son not to get lost. He borrowed a bicycle. He was being very careful with the bicycle because he had borrowed it. As long as he was around the people who lived in the area he knew exactly how to find his way back to the house, so he felt confident. Once he was away from them he got lost. He did not show up when he was supposed to and my aunt started worrying and looking for him. She searched but did not find him. It was getting dark, and my aunt was frustrated and worried about what happened to him.

She had told him to be careful and not get lost, and she was angry at him for not listening to her.

Just before the time that Allen was lost I decided to start home. I was driving by myself and I started to cry for what seemed to be no apparent reason. I felt lost, and even though I read the signs on the freeway they did not seem to make sense even though I had been on this same freeway many, many times before. Nothing looked familiar to me and I became very afraid. I was afraid that my husband was going to be angry at me for getting lost and for being late.

I looked up at a freeway sign and in my emotional state thought it was the right turnoff. Once I had taken it I realized that I had turned on the wrong one. I was heading for the wrong city and definitely not headed home. I became very angry with myself for getting lost. I was angry that I did not listen to something but I was not sure what I thought I was supposed to have listened to. At that point I was *picking up* on my aunt who was angry at my son for being lost. I fluctuated between being afraid and being angry. I was very confused and felt that I was going crazy.

None of this made sense to me. I felt caught in something I did not understand. I was afraid that it was something I could not get out of by myself. When I got to Vallejo (the wrong city) instead of home, I found a telephone booth. I called home and spoke with my husband Ray, and said, "I don't know what is happening to me. I'm lost and I can't find my way home. I haven't been drinking. I'm not 'on' anything, but I can't find my way home."

Ray told me to concentrate on him and he would guide me home. He told me just to keep my thoughts on him and home. He said that he knew exactly what had happened and that he would explain it to me when I got home. By that time I felt a sense of relief knowing that somehow it was going to be okay. I arrived home safely and then I learned the story of Allen's being lost. I had experienced his feelings as well as my aunt's feelings and had walked with both of them emotionally step by step through the entire experience. Just in case you are wondering, Allen also made it home safely.

Ultra-sensitives do have a hard time coping with physical world structure. It is difficult for them to relate to time schedules. It is difficult for them to understand the need for money. They feel stifled in a job in which there is no need for their ultra-sensitivity. This does not mean that ultra-sensitives are not capable of working successfully in the physical world structure. It just means that they feel that the rigidness of the physical structure stops them from being who they are as *feeling* human beings.

Do not assume that ultra-sensitives are unable to learn or do not want to learn. Sometimes they are caught in their emotional patterns and do not know how to get out. To help them get past their obstacles, the first step is to build a bridge of understanding to where they are. Be accepting of what they are experiencing even though you may not understand it from your perception. Ultra-sensitives will get "stuck" in the fact that you do not understand them and they will not be able to move from there.

Once they feel your understanding they will be willing to look at the most negative patterns and be willing to change them. Be sure to take the changes one step at a time. If ultra-sensitives have to look at every single thing that needs to be done to change any pattern, they will be overwhelmed and get "stuck" in the fact that there is too much to do.

You can help with your structural mind by taking them through a step by step process, giving them only the information they need at the moment. If you point out all the ways that they have failed in the past, you will overwhelm them and they will feel hopeless and helpless to do anything for themselves. The best help you can give them is positive and constructive feedback on how to change what is immediately in front of them.

Do not hold back useful or helpful information for fear of hurting them. Yes. Ultra-sensitives are highly emotional, sensitive beings. But remember, they would not have survived this far if they did not have a great deal of strength, courage and stamina within themselves. I often think of an ultra-sensitive that I knew in the past called Cecelia. She was married to a man who loved her very much. Every time he had something to discuss with her that was difficult for him as well as for her, when he would start the discussion she would start crying. He would stop the discussion for fear of hurting her. They kept getting "stuck" in the same place.

I suggested that they continue the discussion— even if Cecelia did start crying—until they reached a conclusion. Her husband learned that even when Cecelia did cry they still could move forward in their discussions. The more they discussed difficult subjects, the less she felt the need to take the full responsiblity, and the more open she was to hearing what she had to change.

She was also more willing to let her husband know what she would like him to change. An ultra-sensitive's nature is to be emotional. This is not wrong nor does it make the ultra-sensitive wrong. It gets in the way of their lives only when they themselves allow their emotions to stand in the way of a full, happy, and fulfilling life.

Sometimes ultra-sensitives will use their emotions as a defense so they do not have to hear what they do not want to hear. You are not helping them by reinforcing that pattern. When you are trying to help ultra-sensitives deal with their negative patterns you cannot speak words with acceptance and openness and at the same time have emotional judgments inside.

WHEN YOU TALK TO ULTRA-SENSITIVES, MAKE SURE YOU HAVE THEIR FULL ATTENTION FIRST

Remember to tell the ultra-sensitive the good s/he is doing. Be sure to reinforce the good. Ultra-sensitives operate from the space that they have to make everything better. They feel they must heal everything, and for this reason they will hear much more clearly what they are doing wrong instead of what they are doing right. Because it is within their nature to fix things, their tendency is to ignore what you have told them about the good they have done, and hear only what they have not done.

When you talk to ultra-sensitives, make sure that you have their full attention first. Many times they will agree with you just to get you out of their "space," and they are actually not listening to you at all.

If they were doing something prior to talking to you and they were intent on what they were doing, chances are that their attention is still on what they were concentrating on and not on what you are saying. Many times if you ask them later to refer back to your conversation, they will not know what you are talking about. As you were talking to them it was not registering in their *communication center* at all.

If you look into the ultra-sensitives' eyes when you are talking to them, you can tell if they are really with you, or if they are only giving you physical attention but not their "mind attention." Many times with the ultra-sensitives I work with, I will look in their eyes to see if they are "home." "Home" means that they are behind their eyes. If there is an empty look, then they are not "home" behind their eyes. It also means that they are not listening to you because they are still caught up in what they were doing. In other words, someone who is looking at them as they were "listening" to you would think that they were listening to you, when in fact their attention is still on what they were working on ten minutes ago.

You can help ultra-sensitives by being understanding and helping them to understand when they are "short-circuited." When too much information comes in too fast for ultra-sensitives to absorb or deal with, they become short-circuited. Too much information coming in on the intellectual, emotional and physical levels will cause a short-circuit.

An intense lack of energy follows a short-circuit, a feeling of loss of connection with the physical-world-reality. A feeling of disconnectedness accompanied by the feeling of being on the brink of losing control, a surrealistic or disconnected feeling from what is happening around the ultra-sensitive follows a short-circuit. Many times ultra-sensitives will hear words and be unable to respond to them. They will hear the sounds but they will be unable to correlate the information they are hearing. The words being spoken to them will not make sense. Many times they will understand the words but be unable to put them together in the expected response. Ultra-sensitives that are short-circuited will have no energy to disagree with anyone about anything. During this time they are likely to make commitments they cannot fulfill.

At the time of short-circuiting, if ultra-sensitives will find a quiet place to rest their mind and think about things, times or places that they love, it will help to center and refill their energy. Saying their name as a centering tool also helps. During a short-circuit it is important not to think about all the things that need to be done. Usually an ultra-sensitive does exactly that during a short-circuit, and that only makes it worse.

Ultra-sensitives should give themselves about fifteen to twenty minutes of rest to regenerate, then they can think about everything that needs to be done. They just need to take a few minutes to gather themselves back together. They need to take time for themselves to do something that fills them instead of something that drains their energy. Be sure, if at all possible, that they get away from people. Even taking twenty minutes for themselves would help.

An "overload" is another energy experience that happens to ultra-sensitives when they have so much on their mind that they are barely holding it together. The overload occurs when one more responsibility that they have to do or think about enters their life. The overload comes when that one last thing is piled on by the ultra-sensitive or by someone else. It feels to the ultra-sensitive as though s/he has folded in the middle like a house of cards.

In this state they need to stay away from people until they can think and relate to them again. They do not even want to answer the simplest questions like, "What color are your eyes?" "Where did you get the dress you are wearing?" "What did you do at work today?" "What would you like to eat?" The ultra-sensitive's reaction is to want to curl up and sleep off the overload. I have found that rest is one of the ways to combat an overload.

Another way to handle an overload is to do something that the ultra-sensitive thinks is fun. Now I do not mean something that the ultra-sensitive can MAKE fun by doing it. I DO mean something that is relaxing and fun to the ultra-sensitive. One of the ways you can help is to plan something for the ultra-sensitive, something that s/he will not have to take charge of in any way. It can be very spontaneous and short range. It could be simply getting away for the moment. Taking a ride and listening to music. Taking a walk in a natural setting. Driving to the ocean, lake, creek or river (as long as s/he enjoys the kind of water you choose and s/he does not have a negative emotional experience connected with it). These will heal the ultra-sensitive. Also, letting them sleep or rest in what they feel is a safe place until they are rejuvenated—this helps. It also helps ultra-sensitives to know that someone is protecting them. It helps them to know that you are shielding them while they rest, until they are regenerated again. They will learn how to protect themselves in the progress of being given a little more to do each time they work on something.

15 *Directing Your Spiritual Sensitive Growth*

How to Know What the Right Path is for You

WHEN YOU BEGIN your spiritual quest or search for knowledge you will find so many opportunities available it may be difficult to know which one is best for you. As you are awakened, there is a deep and driving need to find the right path. You want to do what you are supposed to do. Now that you are aware of all this new knowledge and information you do not want to waste time on the wrong thing. You want to find the right path with determination and dedication. You want to stay on target.

The reason it is called a spiritual "quest" or "search" is that part of the process is the searching. You will grow faster by accepting the fact that you will look into many things and glean what is best for you from all of them. No. I do not recommend that you become a spiritual butterfly, going from flower to flower and not choosing any specific one. What I do recommend is that you look into several different trainings until you find one that you want to dedicate your time, effort and energy to. Once you find what you want to do, stay with that training or development until it no longer challenges you to stretch or reach.

It is time to leave a training when you feel that it is no longer causing you to stretch a little beyond where you feel you can reach; when it no longer makes you feel excited about your development. No matter what training you are in, there will be times when you feel you are not growing; times when you feel that you have learned all you can learn. If you look within yourself during these times, you will also see a resistance to doing what you know that you need to do.

There is no one I know on a spiritual path who once in a while does not just want to stop for a time—to stop reaching, stretching and changing into someone and not being sure who the new "someone" is. At this time all kinds of reasons to quit your training come up. This information is not telling you to quit the training you are in. On the contrary it is telling you that if you are not reaching as much as you need to in order to satisfy yourself, then you are in the well-known slump that happens at times to all seekers. We all look for someone else to push us out of our slump rather than to push ourselves.

During one of these times we can find at least a thousand things wrong with the spiritual training we are currently in, instead of forcing ourselves to move ahead and make a choice to change. If you find yourself judging the training you are in, it means that you are the one that needs to change within yourself. That change may very well be to leave your current training. If you find that nothing excites you about your spiritual training, that nothing in it challenges you to grow, and if you feel that you are not learning anything—then it is time for you to change your training.

You may even feel that you are full and that you have absorbed all you can. This means that you now must take what you have learned out into the world and apply your philosphy to the practical actions of life. It is time to leave so you may apply all you have learned up to that point on your own, with only a limited support system. By having you see what works and also what does not work, you will learn what is missing in your spiritual education. Once you learn this, you can dive back into your concentrated training of spiritual knowledge in order to turn what you have learned into the practical applied knowledge that is called "wisdom." When you are full again the same process takes place.

If you fly from one training to another without applying the new knowledge to your life, then you are what is considered a "spiritual butterfly," flying from one place to another and not allowing yourself to stay any one place long enough to face any of the things that you do not want to face. If you find yourself saying things like, "I don't need that. I've been through that a hundred times or more," that is a judgment that means that you DO need to do what you would rather not do.

You may find yourself saying, "I appreciate the information that is being given in this training but I choose to seek in another direction even though I know there is a lot I could learn by studying in this school of thought." That statement is a choice and observation rather than a judgment because of your willingness to see the good in all things and your openness to acknowledge that there is always something to learn from anything no matter how many times you have heard it. When you feel and speak about a training in this way, it is correct to choose to leave because it is a positive choice to leave at that time with the option to return to it in the future.

Sometimes it takes a thousand times, a thousand times really to hear and receive an "Ah-ha" from information we hear. Sometimes we can also get exactly what we need the first time we hear something. We have both options open to us. The length of time it takes for us to hear what we need to hear in order to change painful patterns depends only on our willingness and acceptance of the information presented.

If you feel "stuck," changing training does not always get you "unstuck." Most of the time you will take the "stuckness" to the next training after the newness of approach or technique is past. You will be facing the same apparent dead-end. What you need to do at that point is to look for what you do NOT want to do next. That is the best way I know to help you to find out what is making you feel so "stuck."

Look at that part of your life you have been avoiding. Is it acquiring knowledge? Going to school? Getting that degree? Maybe it is your physical body. Do you need to get involved in exercise? Does your back need some strengthening or help by exercise or through a chiropractor? Do you need to go into your own business? Are you avoiding your talents in the field of art? Are you avoiding dealing with your emotions because they have always seemed like such a bother? Have you been shelving your emotional sensitivity for a rainy day? If you are not sure what it is, then find someone to help you.

If you want to grow spiritually, then you must attend to physical world things. Once you have them under control you can give them up, but not until they are conquered. You must learn what the rules are and how to live within those rules. Then you must be able to succeed within those rules. Only at that time can you break the rules by saying you do not want to live in the material world.

You can even live the life of a hermit, but only after you have lived among people successfully. You can go away to a mountain top and be a hermit, but sooner or later you will have to face living with people. Something in you will create or demand that you live among people until you have completed whatever it is that you need to complete. If you have already completed with people, then your life as a hermit will be successful.

Everything in life demands a true balance in all things. If you have lived totally in the material world there will be a balance demanded. An event or happening in your life will cause you to see or experience the spiritual world. You will have an experience that will awaken you to the spiritual side of life. It may be a life-threatening crisis to someone you love or to you. It may be an experience that makes you question the life you have led up until now. Not that your life was good or bad, but it may have been an extreme.

When people create extremes in their lives, something within them will trigger the natural course of events that will bring about changes to balance that extreme. Life does not tolerate any extremes for very long. Nature also does not tolerate any extremes. You can watch the weather to prove this out. We will have extreme weather, then the next time that season comes back that extreme will be balanced out.

Sometimes it takes a while, but as I have watched I have found it to be true that everything is always balanced by its equal. The way that we can live the spiritual life is always to seek balance. Balance in the way we live. Balance in the way we talk. Balance in the way we eat, and also in the way we learn, rest, play or teach.

It is important for you to understand that sometimes the right path is a unique combination of many different paths. It may be part of your spiritual development to gather information in order to understand the truth better. If you find yourself reading many different books about spiritual development then accept that for the moment.

You may even have to accept the fact that in this lifetime you are to gather information from many different places to remind you of what you already know. Many times it is true that it is a person's destiny in this life to be a spiritual teacher. They will look in many different places and not be satisfied with any teaching, but just know that they are looking for something; they are just not sure what it is.

What they ARE looking for is acceptance within themselves that they are teachers. Maybe they will have to come across many different teachers in many different places until they can accept the fact that they are supposed to teach. When they take on the responsibility that has been theirs all along, then they feel a sense of being headed in the right direction.

16 *How to Find the Right Spiritual Teacher For Me*

How Can I Find the Right Teacher for Me?

LOOKING FOR THE RIGHT TEACHER can be a confusing and frustrating thing. What do I look for when I am not sure what I want? What qualities do I expect in a teacher? How do I know when it is not the right teacher for me? How do I find someone I can learn from? How do I know that what someone is teaching is right for me? All these questions are ones that all people in their search have asked themselves.

**LOOK FOR A TEACHER WHO WILL SHOW
YOU PARTS OF YOURSELF THAT YOU
COULD NOT REACH ON YOUR OWN**

What do I look for when I am not sure what I want?

Look for persons who are living their beliefs in their life to the best of their abilities. Look for a teacher who makes you think. Look for someone to show you parts of yourself that you could not reach on your own. Find someone who has information that you feel you must have. When there is a drive to learn from someone, then that definitely is the right teacher. When that person can motivate you beyond yourself, then that is the right person to teach you.

Books are a good resource when you are not sure what you are looking for. Keep reading books until you find the information that fits what you want to learn for the moment. Once you have found this information then start asking by using an affirmation on a daily basis. Ask to be led to an excellent teacher who can cause you to learn.

What Qualities do I Expect in a Teacher?

When you are going to learn from someone about your spiritual development, choose someone who you can accept because of the way s/he is applying her/his beliefs to life. Teachers should not ask you to do anything that they are not willing to do or cannot do themselves. Expect your teacher to be human. If s/he had everything accomplished, s/he would not have to be on this physical plane of existence. The fact that s/he is here means that s/he does not have everything done either.

Teachers may be a step or two ahead of you, but you also are a step ahead in areas that they are not accomplished in yet. If you are willing to learn from someone, it means that you have something to teach them also. It may not always be what you think they need to learn. Sometimes the lesson is a lesson of personality traits within them that is within you. Usually it is something both of you need to shed, like a snake shedding its skin: something old that no longer serves either one of you.

Always remember that we all have a right of choice to learn in our own time, so honor your teacher enough to realize that even s/he has to learn in her/his own time as well.

If what your teacher needs to learn upsets you so that you cannot learn from her/him, then you have the wrong teacher for you at that time. That very same teacher may be right for you at a future time, but not right now.

How do I Know That What I am Being Taught is Right for Me?

If what your teacher is teaching is causing you to change your thinking patterns; if what you are learning is causing you to change the way you talk and the words you choose to say; if what you are being taught is making life changes so you or people around you can look back six months and see the changes in you, then you have the right teacher.

You may not always like what you have to do. Many times you will feel that the training is going too slow. You may not want to do the mental disciplines that are required of spiritual development. You may not want to train that part of your mind that has not been trained up until now. Those are just healthy signs of natural resistance within you to the changes that are happening in you. Your teacher should know how to handle them and not take them personally.

Trust your intuition about the trustworthiness of the person that is teaching you. If you are not sure that you want to train with this particular person, then wait. If something does not feel right, then wait until it feels right before you start your training. If the feeling of "not feeling right" goes on for as long as four or five years and you still have not decided on any training at all, that is procrastination. If it feels as though something is missing, it could be that it is a piece of the puzzle that you have not fitted together yet. It could also be that the training that you are looking at is missing something in order to be the right one for you.

UNCONDITIONAL LOVE MOVES ANYTHING THAT NEEDS TO BE MOVED WITHIN US OR WITHIN THE WORLD

Do not allow any person that calls her/himself a teacher to degrade you in any way. Sometimes in training we become locked in and a teacher needs to shake us out of our blocked place. There are many ways to help a student out of a blocked place without being abusive. There is no need to take actions that take away another person's dignity. There are embarrassing moments in everyone's life, but abuse of any kind to the student is not necessary to learning. In fact it retards learning. I feel very strongly that UNCONDITIONAL LOVE moves anything that needs to be moved within us or within the world.

If you have an ideal of what you believe a Master Teacher is, the best way you can help yourself and help your teacher to cause you to learn is to get rid of those "positive judgments." Your judgments are your perceptions of what an ideal Master Teacher is. Let the teacher you find be in the ongoing process of mastering her/his skills. Let your teacher be a Master at helping you apply a wisdom that is ever changing to fit your needs to grow in your personal development.

Your preconceived ideas of what you believe a Master Teacher should be will only get in your way and in your teacher's way of creating movement in your spiritual development. If you believe a teacher must be only the way you believe a teacher must be, then you have given your teacher no place to help you grow and expand.

If someone is on this earth s/he is either moving INTO growing spiritually, moving OUT of growing spiritually, or growing spiritually. That is the trinity of development. That is true of any kind of teacher you may have whether physical, academic, emotional or spiritual. Even if your teacher does not seem to you to be growing or changing at all, remember that development does not always show on the outside immediately.

Development is like a seed growing in the earth. A lot of the growth happens within the earth unseen. Then when it breaks through the earth it can be seen by you and by others. Be patient with yourself when it feels as though you are doing a lot of work but you have nothing to show for it. This is the time to trust that all the work you are doing is causing movement and change. The change happens first within you before it breaks through from inside and shows on the outside.

As an ultra-sensitive it is important for you to understand spiritual ethics. There is a spiritual ethics code that you live by whether you know the code or not. It is like a baby who lives with electricity but has little awareness of it and does not understand it. The baby may put a safety pin in the electrical socket and get shocked even though s/he did not know or understand about electricity.

Once you awaken to the spiritual ethics code you must be responsible for living it from that moment on. As an adult you must not take an electrical appliance into the bath with you. If you do, knowing what will happen to you, you take the chance of being electrically burned or worse. Once you have awakened to the knowledge, breaking the code will cause the repercussions to come back to you tenfold.

Spiritual Ethics

1. I have no right to interfere in anyone's life even for their own good. If I do, then I must accept their karma as part of my life until I release the need to

interfere and have balanced the karma I created by my interference.

2. I have to ask permission to work with anyone. I must have the person's verbal agreement to work with her/him on a spiritual level. If I do not have her/his agreement, then I have accepted her/his karma to whatever degree that I have interfered, as long as I do not have permission. If it is for a baby, or persons who are unable to speak for themselves, then I must have permission from the responsible adult.

3. If I want something that someone else has, I must ask that they receive exactly what they want or better. Then I must also ask that I receive what I am asking for only if it is for my highest good and the highest good of all concerned. I must ask for a better job or a better relationship for them, remembering that I have to ask permission to work with anyone.

4. As an ultra-sensitive I will not broadcast my out-of-control emotions in a group of ultra-sensitives or anywhere just because I feel safe or feel they deserve to know how I feel. More and more I will bring my emotions under my control (but not suppress them) and expand my sensitivity to its full strength and universal potential.

17 Is There A Difference Between Psychic (Intuitive) and Spiritual?

IT IS IMPORTANT to understand the meaning of the words that are used to discuss "psychic" energy and spirituality, namely "psychic" (intuitive) and "spiritual." I have studied the meaning of many words used by people who feel they are spiritually based, and I have found that often they do not include these two words as part of "spirituality." I have found other spiritual people, however, who DO include these words as an integral part of their spiritual focus.

By studying the words used by both groups, I have also discovered that all the words used in the discussion of "spirituality" and "psychic (intuitive) skills" are interrelated. The only time they APPEAR to be in opposition is when individuals inject their own personal interpretation into them or, out of personal bias, separate them.

There are spiritual teachers who stress the strict avoidance of using one's intuitive skills, maintaining that doing so will block one's spiritual development. I have not found this to be true. On the other hand, I have found that my intuitive abilities *enhance* my spiritual life.

If people are willing to see the wholeness of the word "psychic" (intuitive), they will see that it is just one spoke on the wheel of spiritual development worth no more or no less than any other spoke of the spiritual wheel of truth.

ALL THINGS BIG AND SMALL IN THIS UNIVERSE ARE SPIRITUAL, NO MATTER HOW MANY TIMES WE CAUSE THEM TO BE DIVIDED BY OUR INTELLECT OR OUR EMOTIONAL FEARS

One of the ways that a person can grow and learn spiritually is to integrate intuitive skills openly into her/his life as spiritual tools and understand that intuitive energies or abilities are a PART of spirituality and cannot in truth be separated even if some people do use words to separate "psychic" (intuitive) and "spiritual" into opposites rather than seeing them as the complements they are. All things big and small in this universe are spiritual, no matter how many times we cause them to be divided by our intellect or our emotional fears.

What is "Spirit?" "Spirit" is the vitalized breath in your body. It is the breath that is created with the highest integrity and conscious thought while breathing. Spirit is the vigor and life force that moves your body, your brain, your consciousness and unconsciousness. Spirit is your soul. Spirit is the thinking, motivating, feeling part of human beings. It is often distinguished from the body, brain or intelligence.

SPIRIT is the intuitive or feminine, and *MATTER* is the intellectual or masculine. Spirit is the action that manifests in human beings against all odds and against the reasoning that says something cannot be done. Spirit goes beyond reason and proves that it CAN be done. Spirit is life. Spirit is your will to live and work against all obstacles. Spirit is the vital energy that causes a body to move, live, breathe, and talk. Spirit is regarded as being separate from matter, yet it brings life to matter.

What is "Spiritual?" "Spiritual" means a nature that exists and shows a more refined state of being because of its contact with spirit. People can work and continue to do even greater work on themselves because of the connection with their spirit, until they are pure of heart. Spiritual work is work that is done by people upon themselves that does not always show a tangible or material result in the beginning. Eventually their lives show the results of that spiritual work by their example, not by just their words. Spiritual is something or someone that has a holy nature because of spirit. Spirit can be described as your soul.

"Spiritual" is also a process that refines the material world part of people because of their spirit's contact and connection with them. If SPIRIT is the thinking, motivating, feeling part of human beings, then SPIRITUAL is the result of that thinking. Spiritual is the manifestion of the motivation and the reaching out and touching with feelings whether they take the form of spoken words, spiritual ideas in thought, or Spirit expressed by action.

"Spiritual" is something that is not measureable or tangible in the physical world, yet it affects and touches our lives more deeply than anything made of matter on this physical earth. As human beings we have a tendency to discount anything that we cannot prove to be real by all the things we use for measurement on this planet. We as human beings seem to need the security of being able to prove the same thing over and over in order for it to be believeable or acceptable in the intellectual scheme of things. Yet we keep striving for the meaning to life and the meaning to our life because there is a part of each of us that knows that there is more to life than what we physically experience. Living the spiritual life is living or having a belief in the Divine Essence in all things in the Universe.

"Universe" means our personal universe—body, mind and spirit, as well as the physical universe we live in. "Spiritual" has to do with the soul. The soul itself cannot be described or defined by physical scientific laws because it is not tangible or physical, yet it can affect our physical body and our physical external world.

Living the spiritual life means to live your life with conscious awareness of all life while in the process of developing your total ability to live in the now; living your life knowing that all things that exist are precious.

What is the spiritual life and who is growing spiritually? Everyone on this planet is growing spiritually (whether they are aware of it or not), even though they may not be using the recognized terms that people on the spiritual path are using. If people are ON this planet, they are involved in spiritual development because everything is God. Everything is spiritual development. It appears otherwise only because some people are moving at different speeds than others. It is only ego to assume that because you are awakened to the quickening of your spiritual self that others who have not awakened yet are not growing. Consciously living the spiritual life with growing awareness is the spiritual realization of applied personal growth that moves in a spiral pattern.

IT IS ONLY EGO TO ASSUME THAT BECAUSE YOU ARE AWAKENED TO THE QUICKENING OF YOUR SPIRITUAL SELF THAT OTHERS WHO HAVE NOT AWAKENED YET ARE NOT GROWING

Spiritual growth is the movement you create when you make an in-depth change in any area of your life. The change you make within yourself reacts in you and then moves outward from your personal nucleus to form a circling spiral. That spiral goes on to form a series of constantly changing planes within you that effect changes in you, the loved ones around you, and your world.

The words "spirit," "spiritual," "psychic," and "intuitive" involve intangibles. What is "psychic?" "Psychic" is of or having to do with psyche, or mind/soul. "Psychic" is something beyond known natural or known physical processes. It is also used to define someone who is ultra-sensitive to forces beyond the physical world. The word "psychic" was taken from the word "psyche"; to me it means the conceptual language of the psyche or soul. "Psychic" (intuition) is the ability to sense and receive information beyond what is fully known to our mind at the present time. It is a natural process that we are meant to utilize in our daily life.

SPIRITUAL GROWTH IS THE MOVEMENT YOU CREATE WHEN YOU MAKE AN IN-DEPTH CHANGE IN ANY AREA OF YOUR LIFE THAT BRINGS YOU CLOSER TO THE DIVINE

It is there to help us sense danger to ourselves and to those we love. Instead of using the word "psychic," which many people attach to "supernatural," I use the term "ultra-sensitive." "Ultra-sensitive" defines a person who can sense things that others cannot sense and is ultra-sensitive to things that cannot be measured by science at the present time.

Instead of using the words "psychic abilities," I have used the word "intuition" throughout the book except in this chapter. In this chapter I want to correlate the words "psychic" and "intuition." It is the noun ("a" psychic) and not the verb ("to be" intuitive/ psychic) that has the stigma. "Intuition" is a more wholistic word that truly describes what happens to ultra-sensitives when they are experiencing their ultra-sensitivity.

"Intuition" means the act or faculty of knowing without the use of rational processes. It is the immediate understanding of something not evident or deducible. It can also mean the capacity for guessing accurately or having sharp insight. Remember how many times you used the word "guess" to predict a future event . . . and then it came true? You thought you were making it up when in actuality you were making a prediction. "Guess" means to predict (a result or event) without sufficient tangible information.

The more we use our intuition AS THE NATURAL ABILITY IT IS (in the same way we use our hands, nose or eyes), the less fear and misunderstanding there will be in our world. It is our responsibility to use all the resources that we have available to make our world a better place. Our intuition is just one of those resources, and is no more or no less important than any of our other resources.

Spirit is the thinking, motivating, feeling part of human beings. It is often distinguished from the body, brain or intelligence (reason). *Intuition* is of the spirit and is created to help us to protect ourselves, our loved ones and our world. When this ability is refined, purified and made holy it then becomes a spiritual tool for the good of all, including the medium who is the person that is the channel for spiritual energy to travel through.

In learning the definition of the words that are used in connection with spiritual and psychic development it has been discovered that all things connected with spiritual are refined and purified knowledge that must be applied to your life for the highest good of others as well as yourself. It is important not to get caught up in the intellectual meaning of the words but rather to apply the words to your life and connect with your spiritual development through your heart center. You must believe in yourself and trust what you feel first and foremost above all things because your God-Self is centered in your heart. Trust in your God-Self and all things shall be clear and truth shall be yours to live your life fully and completely. If it feels correct to use your intuitive abilities, then by all means add them to the sum total of your being. If you do not want to use your intuitive skills, then allow yourself to set them aside until (or if) they ripen and become an integrated part of your life. Any time you take intuitive skills out of context with your spiritual development, you are putting yourself on a path that will cause you to become caught up in side issues of psychic phenomena that will delay your spiritual development. As long as your intuitive abilities are a part of your spiritual development and they are no more and no less important than any other part of your being, then your intuitive skills will be an asset in your search for truth.

18 *Universal Laws*

UNIVERSAL LAWS ARE laws that work for people around the world. Universal laws are laws that have no personal interpretation within them. They are laws that work for all people and not in just one country, state, city or community. They change as our consciousness changes in the world collectively. Universal laws make us think beyond ourselves and our personal lives. Understanding them and living by them can create peace throughout the world. There are many more universal laws than the ones I am stating here, but this is a start. My interpretations are just a basis, a beginning for you to begin thinking about why these laws are so important to us in our lives.

1. There is nothing permanent in the universe but change.

The one thing we can count on as sensitives is the fact that everything is changing. When we are having a wonderful time, that is changing. When we are having a hard time, that is changing. The weather is changing. The cycles are changing. The earth is changing. While we are experiencing ANYTHING it is in the process of change right at that moment. Our bodies are changing. Our consciousness is changing. Nothing is permanent except change.

2. That which is above is also below.

Whatever is happening in one area of your life is also happening in other areas. If something is happening in your body then it is also happening to your intellect, your emotions and your spirit. There is no isolated effect in your body, mind or spirit. If one area is affected then other areas are also affected.

3. You own nothing and no one, but everything is yours.

You can live by the physical laws of the land. You can buy land and own possessions. But in fact you really own none of them because their value and worth do not transfer to the spiritual plane of eternal existence. Everything is yours because you are a part of everything.

The same energy that is in you is also in everything—animate and inanimate, no matter what it is. Because you began from the same energy, you can create anything you want and you can have everything. It can be yours to manifest as you will.

4. What you send out comes back to you: The Law of Cause and Effect.

The Law of Cause and Effect means that for every action there is a reaction. Whatever you do has an effect on everyone and everything. There are no isolated incidents; there is only balance in the universe. There is only action and the effects of that action.

5. History repeats itself until an event or thing is completed in our experience.

Our personal history repeats itself until we understand what we are doing and change our actions or reactions to another person, ourselves, or life in general.

Epilogue

THIS BOOK IS only the beginning. There is so much more knowledge and information to recognize and acknowledge within ourselves as ultra-sensitives, and there are so many more kinds of ultra-sensitivity to discover. We need more knowledge and training in order to enable us to recognize the ways in which ultra-sensitivity affects our lives each and every day. We must stop blocking information and denying those things we don't understand, concluding that because we don't understand them, they have no value. Also, many young children who are ultra-sensitive and have a magnetic, healing energy, are unnecessarily hurt when they attract people who need their healing, but through a lack of understanding—by the person as well as the child—both end up in pain.

I want to hear from you. Please write and let me know what your talents are. If you are not sure, then write and share with me the experiences you may have suffered as a result of your being ultra-sensitive. Help *me* to rediscover emotional as well as intuitive gifts in ultra-sensitivity so we can create a healthier world for tomorrow by being happy, well-balanced ultra-sensitives. If you are uncertain whether or not you are an ultra-sensitive, write anyway and tell me about events or circumstances in your life that you do not understand. Let us learn to heal ourselves together by creating a deeper understanding of who we are.

Write:

Marcy Calhoun
861 Gray Avenue, Suite N • Yuba City, CA 95991
Message phone: (916) 755-4822

Please enclose a self-addressed stamped envelope for reply.

About the Author

MARCY CALHOUN is a psychic practitioner. For nineteen years she has been teaching people how to integrate psychic and spiritual skills. Marcy has presented lectures on "How to Trust your Feelings" and has taught classes on what she calls "Psychic Self-defense." Currently she is giving classes as well as "Breaking Through" workshops. Marcy maintains a private practice in psychic counseling throughout California and in Seattle, Washington. She has two children and lives with her husband in the Sierra foothills of California.